D1524286

RETRIEVING REALISM

RETRIEVING REALISM

HUBERT DREYFUS ✦ CHARLES TAYLOR

 Harvard University Press

Cambridge, Massachusetts
London, England
2015

Second printing

Library of Congress Cataloging-in-Publication Data

Dreyfus, Hubert L.
  Retrieving realism / Hubert Dreyfus, Charles Taylor.
    pages cm
  Includes bibliographical references and index.
  ISBN 978-0-674-96751-9
  1. Knowledge, Theory of. 2. Realism. I. Taylor, Charles, 1931– II. Title.
  BD161.D74 2015
  121—dc23
  2014042255

In memory of Samuel Todes

Contents

Preface

This book started when we were together during a three-week study residence in Bellagio, and we want to express our profound gratitude to the Rockefeller Foundation for launching us on this path.

We want to thank all our discussion partners, mainly the many scholars who were involved in the Dreyfus-McDowell debate.

In particular, there is one person—Richard Rorty, friend, adversary, and sparring partner—whose objections did much to improve our argument, and whose untimely death prevented him from poking holes in our final version. This is just one of the many reasons why he is sorely missed today.

We also want to remember another friend, Samuel Todes, whose pathbreaking work has informed our thinking. Perhaps this book might help bring attention to his important contribution to the issues we discuss.

We would also like to thank Geneviève Dreyfus and Muhammad Velji for their invaluable help in preparing the final manuscript, and again Muhammad Velji for his invaluable work in drawing up the Index.

Portions of Chapters 1 and 2 were published in *Mind, Reason, and Being-in-the-World: The McDowell-Dreyfus Debate*, edited by Joseph K. Schear (London: Routledge, 2013), Chapter 3.

RETRIEVING REALISM

CHAPTER ONE

A Picture Held Us Captive

"A PICTURE HELD US CAPTIVE" (*Ein Bild hielt uns gefangen*). So speaks Wittgenstein in paragraph 115 of the *Philosophical Investigations*.[1] What he is referring to is the powerful picture of mind-in-world which inhabits and underlies what we could call the modern epistemological tradition, which begins with Descartes. The point he wants to convey with the use of the word "picture" (*Bild*) is that there is something here different and deeper than a theory. It is a largely unreflected-upon background understanding which provides the context for, and thus influences all our theorizing in, this area. The claim could be interpreted as saying that mainline epistemological thinking, which descends from Descartes, has been contained within and

1. Ludwig Wittgenstein, *Philosophical Investigations*, trans. G. E. M. Anscombe (Oxford: Blackwell, 1997), 48. The actual text of para 115 reads: "A *picture* held us captive. And we could not get outside it, for it lay in our language and language seemed to repeat it to us inexorably." (*Ein Bild hielt uns gefangen. Und heraus konnten wir nicht, denn es lag in unsrer Sprache, und sie schien es uns unerbittlich zu wiederholen.*) In our discussion, we argue more that the picture is anchored in our whole way of thinking, our way of objectifying the world, and thus our way of life, and therefore also in our language.

hence shaped by this not fully explicit picture; that this has been a kind of captivity, because it has prevented us from seeing what is wrong with this whole line of thought. At certain points, we are unable to think "outside the box," because the picture seems so obvious, so commonsensical, so unchallengeable.[2]

To identify the picture would be to grasp a big mistake, something like a framework mistake, which distorts our understanding, and at the same time prevents us from seeing this distortion for what it is.

We think Wittgenstein was right about this. There is a big mistake operating in our culture, a kind of operative (mis)understanding of what it is to know, which has had dire effects on both theory and practice in a host of domains. To sum it up in a pithy formula, we might say that we (mis)understand knowledge as "mediational." In its original form, this emerged in the idea that we grasp external reality through internal representations. Descartes, in one of his letters, declared himself "certain that I can have no knowledge of what is outside me except by means of the ideas I have within me" (*assuré que je ne puis avoir aucune connaissance de ce qui est hors de moi, que par l'entremise des idées que j'ai eu en moi*).[3] This sentence makes sense against a certain topology of mind and world. The reality I want to know is outside the mind; my knowledge of it is within. This knowledge consists in states of mind which purport to represent accurately what is out there. When they do correctly and reliably represent this reality, then there is knowledge. I have knowledge of things only through ("by means of" [*par l'entremise de*]) these inner states, which we can call "ideas."

We want to call this picture "mediational" because of the force of the claim which emerges in the crucial phrase "only through." In knowledge I have a kind of contact with outer reality, but I get this only through some inner states. One crucial aspect of the picture which is being taken as given

---

2. Wittgenstein actually says in this paragraph that the grammar of our language endlessly repeats the picture to us, and that's why it is so hard to escape. We think this sense of what is implicit in grammar actually depends on something more complex in our background understanding of mind, agency, and world. It is the aim of this book to explain this dependency further.

3. Rene Descartes, "Letter to Gibieuf of 19 January 1642," in *The Philosophical Works of Descartes*, vol. 3, trans. John Cottingham et al. (Cambridge: Cambridge University Press, 1991), 201.

here, and is thus on the road to being hardened into an unchallengeable context, is the inner-outer structure. The reality we seek to grasp is outside; the states whereby we seek to grasp it are inside. The mediating elements here are "ideas," inner representations; and so the picture in this variant could be called "representational." But this, as we shall see, is not the only variant. This particular version has been challenged, but what has often escaped attention is the deeper topology which gives the unnoticed context for both the original version and the challenges.

This last point is the hardest one to make convincing. In all sorts of ways, Descartes passes in contemporary philosophy for a much-refuted thinker. His way of making the inner-outer distinction was via a radical differentiation between physical and mental substances, and this dualism has very few defenders today. Moreover, the mediating element, the idea, this particulate content of the mind, available to introspection, seems dubious, and worse, irrelevant to most contemporary accounts of knowledge. And one could go on in the litany of rejections.

And yet, something essential remains. Take the "linguistic turn." For many philosophers today, if we wanted to give the contents of the mind, we should have recourse not to little images in the mind, but rather to something like sentences held true by an agent, or more colloquially the person's beliefs. This shift is important, but it keeps the mediational structure intact. The mediating element is no longer something psychic, but rather "linguistic." This allows it in a way to be "outside," in the sense of the Cartesian distinction, because sentences circulate in public space, between speakers. But in another way, in that the sentence's being held true is a fact about individual speakers, and their (often unvoiced) thoughts, we re-create the same basic pattern: the reality is out there, and the holdings true are in minds; we have knowledge when these beliefs (sentences held true) reliably correspond to the reality; we have knowledge through the beliefs. (Knowledge is "justified, true belief.")

Then take the materialist turn. We deny Cartesian dualism by denying one of its terms. There is no "mental substance," everything is matter, and thinking itself arises out of matter. This is the kind of position which Quine espoused, for instance. And yet Quine re-created a similar structure in the new metaphysical context. Our knowledge comes to us through "surface irritations," the points in our receptors where the various stimuli from the environment impinge. It is these which are the basis of our knowledge.

Alternatively, he sometimes takes the immediate description of what is impinging, observation sentences, as basic, and he sees the edifice of science as built under the requirement that shows how (most of) these hold. In either variant, there is a mediational, or "only through," structure here. The proof of the indeterminacy of translation, of the uncertainty of reference, of the plurality of scientific accounts comes from considerations that the choice between different ontological or scientific postulates will always remain not fully determined by these basic starting points.

"Inner" is being given a materialist sense here, in this "naturalized epistemology." Our knowledge of the external world comes in "through" the receptors, and so they define the boundary, only in a "scientific," and not a "metaphysical," way. Similarly, we see the Cartesian structure repeated in various conjectures about a brain in a vat, which might be fooled into thinking that it was really in an embodied agent in a world, as long as a fiendish scientist was giving it the right input. Just as the old epistemology worried that as long as the contents of our minds remain the same, some evil demon might be controlling the input so that the world could change without our being any the wiser, so contemporaries re-edit a structurally similar nightmare concerning the brain. This has become the material replacement of the mind, supposedly because it is what causally underlies thinking. The mediational structure, and the mediating interface of inputs (now controlled by the fiendish scientist), and hence a parallel "only through" claim, all survive the "materialist" transposition.

If one asks the proponent of the brain-in-the-vat hypothesis why he focuses on the brain, he will reply something to the effect that thinking "supervenes on" the brain. But how does he know this? How do we know that you don't need more than the brain, maybe the brain and nervous system, or maybe even the whole organism, or (more likely) the whole organism in its environment, in order to get what we understand as perception and thinking? The answer is that no one knows. The brain-in-the-vat hypothesis only looks plausible because of the force of the mediational structure, our captivity in the picture implicit in modern epistemology, which requires something to play the role of "inside."

Let's take another transposition, the critical turn. We mean the shift inaugurated by Kant. Here the basic relation is no longer the picture-like internal representation and outer reality. Rather, what Kant calls "representation" (*Vorstellung*) often seems to be the same as outer (empirical) reality. But in any case, the stuff of intuition for Kant comes in another sense from "outside," in that it is something we receive, as we are "affected" (*affiziert*) by things, in contrast to what is shaped by the categories which are the products of our minds. The "only through" claim here takes a rather different form. It is only through the shaping of the categories that our intuitions furnish objects for us, that there is experience and knowledge. Without the concepts which we provide, intuition would be "blind." "Inner," "outer," and "only through" all take on new meanings (indeed, in the case of the first two, more than one meaning) in Kant's work. But the basic structure survives. That the continuity here is a significant and fateful one will emerge later in the discussion.

We can already see that the underlying picture of epistemology still holds a lot more captives than the critics of Cartesian dualism, or mentalism, or "foundationalism" usually realize. Indeed, it holds many of these very critics in its thrall. We shall see later that even many who declare themselves "postmoderns" have not escaped the prison. We hope this will become evident later in the argument. But for the moment we should just bear in mind that various forms of skepticism about the powers of the mind and the reach of science have not been absent from the tradition. It was born in an argument against skepticism (Descartes); and it has had its famous skeptical turns (Hume, not to speak of Quine's ontological relativity). Why this had to be so will be discussed later. For the moment, we must be content with the hints at a deep continuity which we have offered in the preceding paragraphs.

1

The connection between skepticism and modern epistemology is plain at the very beginning, in the work of Descartes. He uses skepticism, we might say, not to further a skeptic's agenda, but to establish his own topology of self, mind, and world. The reader is bludgeoned in the first *Meditation* with the full barrage of skeptical argument. The point is not, as with the ancients, or more recently Montaigne, to get us to realize how little we know. On the contrary, the argument will end with the most daring and far-reaching claims to certainty. The strategic point of these opening arguments is to force us to distinguish between inner and outer, between the reality of bodily things and that of the contents of the mind. When we realize how vulnerable our supposedly reliable knowledge of external reality is to skeptical arguments, and then later come to see that what we cannot doubt is the content of our own "ideas," we will be cured forever of that muddled elision of bodily and mental, which arises from the substantial union of body and mind, but which is the major source of obscure and confused thought.

This major difference of strategic goal is what marks Descartes off from his sources for *Meditation I*, the ancient thinkers of the Pyrrhonian tradition. Descartes' assimilation of their arguments has led us to forget how different was their enterprise, even though some near contemporaries, like Montaigne, were still in continuity with ancient thought, and even though, one might add, there was a partial recovery of this older way of thinking with Hume.

The point of ancient skepticism was to show us how little we really could claim to know. For every type of claim to knowledge, a counterclaim could be made to seem plausible. Do we think we can be sure of the existence of physical objects around us? Well how about the stick which looks bent in water? and so on. In all these cases, reflection shows us that the issue is ultimately undecidable. *Isostheneia* reigns; that is, both sides are equally weak. So you can't have real knowledge.

What was the point of showing this? Our goal in life is serenity, a state of *ataraxia* or untroubledness. But to achieve this, we have to give up on unattainable goals, like sure science. But don't we need some knowledge of things to go about living our lives? This was the criticism which seems to have occurred frequently to nonphilosophers in the ancient world, if we judge by the stories of philosophers who bumped into walls, or fell into wells. The skeptic's answer was that we have all that we need in the way things look to us. If we follow these appearances, we will usually fare well. We don't need to seek on top of this some scientific certainty that the appearances track "reality."

Not only do we not need this, and not only will it needlessly agitate us to try vainly to seek it, but Sextus argues that such knowledge, were we to have it, would only disturb our serenity. His claim is that any belief that something is by nature good or bad leads to perturbation, making us want it when we don't have it, and fear losing it when we do. Of course, you can be cold or thirsty, but you make things worse by opining that what you suffer is evil by nature.[4]

---

4. Leo Groarke, *Greek Scepticism: Anti-Realist Trends in Ancient Thought* (Montreal: McGill-Queen's University Press, 1990), 134.

What these arguments do for you is that they bring about a kind of conversion, whereby from an anxious seeker after truth, you become capable of suspending judgement, and then living without scientific certainty, *adoxastas.*

The "appearances" here being appealed to can easily be identified with Descartes' "ideas." But this is a mistake, as Burnyeat argues.[5] This is because "appearances" don't make up an ontologically defined class, over against realities. They are more like the way things look to us at some moment than a particular kind of mental content. Indeed, there is no need to place this way-things-look in the mind at all. The stick looking bent in water could be equally seen as a feature of sticks-in-water. Or else the appearance can be the way we feel as ensouled bodies, cold, hot, in pain, etc. *Phainomena* and *phantasiai* don't always mean sensibles (*aisthêta*). For they cover, for example, the *phantasia* that not all *phantasiai* are true, or the conclusion of the skeptics' argument that everything is relative.[6]

The distinction applies to the supposed epistemic status of how things look, whether they ever deserve the more honorific condition of real knowledge. It doesn't establish *phantasiai* as a particular kind of entity. But this is exactly what Descartes sets out to do. It is crucial to his argument to establish "ideas" as a particular kind of inner, mental entity, which are marked out from the external ones in that they are in certain respects immune to skeptical argument. It is an important stage in Descartes' argument to show that one can have certain knowledge about appearances. That is why the ontological indeterminacy of the ancient *phantasia* has to be cleared up. My feeling cold or hot or in pain has to be ontologically segmented into an external, physical condition of low or high temperature, or tissue damage, on one hand, and some inner, purely mental impression on the other. Descartes replaces the traditional ancient topology of the soul, which is tripartite—*aesthêsis, phantasia, nous* (sensation, imagination, intellect [*entendement*])—with the new single chamber in which everything appears together. Rorty describes this as the "notion of a single inner space in which bodily and perceptual sensations . . . mathematical truths, moral rules, the idea of

5. I have drawn on Miles Burnyeat's discussion here; see Miles Burnyeat, "Can the Skeptic Live with His Skepticism?" and "Idealism & Greek Philosophy," in *Idealism Past and Present*, ed. G. Vesey (Cambridge: Cambridge University Press, 1982).

6. Burnyeat, "Can the Skeptic," 121.

God, moods of depression, and all the rest of what we now call 'mental' were objects of quasi-observation."[7]

This corresponds to the new generic term *cogitare*, or *penser*, which subsumes the full range of psychic states beneath it: "What is a thing that thinks? A thing that doubts, understands, affirms, denies, is willing, is unwilling, and also imagines and has sensory perceptions." (*Qu'est-ce qu'une chose qui pense? Cest-à-dire une chose qui doute, qui conçoit, qui affirme, qui nie, qui veut, qui ne veut pas, qui imagine aussi, et qui sent.*)[8] The senses and imagination are now distinguished in that they are the source of some of these *cogitationes* and not others, and realizing this shows us how to treat them, and what confidence we should place in them. But there is only one locus where all appear.

By the same token this single locus is radically distinct from the body, where the ancient loci were distinguished by their greater or lesser degree of interpenetration with our bodily existence. A new and radical dualism has been established, which we want to call in the further stages of our argument the "dualist sorting."

Why is this important for Descartes' strategy? Because by carving out ideas as a particular kind of thing, one whose *esse* is *percipi*, that is, whose basic mode of existence is to appear to us "inwardly," we isolate a kind of entity about which we can be certain. We stop the rot of skepticism, the endless retreat before the fact of *isostheneia*; we arrive at a firm footing: at least this is indubitable. And the point of that is to provide a foundation for returning to reconquer some of the territory seemingly ceded in the first *Meditation*. Descartes, like General MacArthur, finds his safe haven, his Australia, from which his vow to return can be fulfilled. For via the *cogito*, and then the proof of the existence of God, we move from the undeniable fact of our having certain ideas to certainty in a scientifically established order of external things. Skepticism turns out to undercut itself, once it is used to establish the new dualism between inner and outer, and hence the new terrain of the inner, whose contents are (supposedly) immune to skeptical

7. Richard Rorty, *Philosophy and the Mirror of Nature* (Princeton, NJ: Princeton University Press, 2009), 50.

8. Rene Descartes, "*Meditations*, II, Adam and Tannery, IX-1, 278," in *The Philosophical Works of Descartes*, vol. 2, trans. John Cottingham et al. (Cambridge: Cambridge University Press, 1984), 19.

argument. Nothing further from the ancient (or Montaignian) agenda could be conceived.

This is one of the motivations for the invention of the new kind of entity, the "idea." But this was also over-overdetermined. It came to be not only because of the role it was destined to play in a foundationalist enterprise, but also under the influence of the mechanization of the world picture which was coming about through the work of Galileo and other agents of the scientific revolution. Perception, considered as a process in material nature, could best be conceived as the impression created in the mind by surrounding reality. As Locke later put it, ideas "are produced in us . . . by the operation of insensible particles on the senses."[9] From this point of view, the idea is the first effect that this process of impinging makes on the mind, prior to any combinations or connections which the mind itself sets up. It is what the mind receives purely passively, the "impression" made on it, to use the expression later introduced by Hume. Again, in Locke's terms: "In this part the understanding is merely passive; and whether or not it will have these beginnings, and as it were materials of knowledge, is not in its own power."[10]

Mechanistic explanation provided a place for this entity, the passive impression. This was how it was defined in the causal account. But the strategic account, in terms of the foundationalist enterprise, also needed an entity of this kind. It defined the point where the project of foundationalist reconstruction of knowledge could start. On the strategic account the basic idea (later called by Locke the "simple idea") was the content that could not itself be construed as the product of interpretation or inference by the mind. For if so, one would have to dig down farther to what was interpreted or inferred from in order to get solid foundations. On the causal account, this same idea was seen as purely passively received, a bare impression. The given prior to interpretation and the passively received come together as two sides of the same entity, two ways of describing its basic nature. Causal passivity and freedom from interpretation are taken as two descriptions of the same condition. This is the basis of what was later called the Myth of the (purely)

9. John Locke, *An Essay Concerning Human Understanding*, ed. P. H. Nidditch (Oxford: Clarendon Press, 1975), 2.8.13. In 4.2.11, Locke speaks of "globules."

10. Ibid., 2.1.25. See also 2.30.3, where Locke says that the mind is "wholly passive in respect of its simple ideas," and 2.2.2, where he says that it is not in our power to create or to destroy a simple idea.

Given,[11] and of all the confusions between the "space of causes" and the "space of reasons" which this involved. It also amounts to a reification of thinking.[12]

2

This dualist theory of representation, of knowledge as the inner depiction of outer reality, which we see crystallizing in the seventeenth century with Descartes and Locke, is the origin of what we're calling the tradition of mediational epistemology. We're arguing that this is an important tradition here, whose members are bound together by a certain picture (*Bild*) of mind-in-world, even though they are in vigorous disagreement with each other on many issues, and even though contemporary members see themselves as totally liberated from the thrall of Cartesianism.

What then is this picture? Otherwise put, what are the elements of continuity, which straddle all the differences, even those which seem to contemporaries so vital? We want to identify four interwoven strands. In certain cases, one or another of these may be broken, but the continuity is maintained by the rest.

1. The first is the "only through" structure, the one which justifies the title "mediational": our knowledge of, or access to, the world "outside" us, beyond the boundaries of the mind/organism, comes about only through some features in the mind/organism. These can be seen as representations or depictions, either ideas, or beliefs, or sentences held true. Or they can be seen, following the critical tradition, as categorial forms, ways we have of

11. The phrase is from Wilfrid Sellars, "Empiricism and the Philosophy of Mind," in *Science, Perception, and Reality* (London: Routledge & Kegan Paul, 1968), 196.

12. This is most clearly evident in Locke, who pushes the metaphor of construction out of building materials to the utmost in his account of the operations of the mind. Ideas are "materials," and man's "power, however managed by art and skill, reaches no farther than to compound and divide the materials that are made to his hand" (2.2.2). And after speaking of the formation of complex ideas out of simple ones, Locke says: "This shows man's power, and its ways of operation, to be much the same in the material and intellectual world. For the materials in both being such as he has no power over, either to make or to destroy, all that man can do is either to unite them together, or to set them by one another, or wholly separate them" (2.12.1).

conceptually structuring the input, of making sense of it for ourselves. Often these two combine, in the notion that our depictions of outer reality are inescapably structured by the categories which either emerge from our nature or have developed over time. In either case, the epistemic relation to the surrounding world only exists in and through these forms and/or depictions.

2. It is a normal implication of this mediational picture that the content of our knowledge can be analyzed into clearly defined, explicit elements. It consists of "ideas" which we have assembled, in the Cartesian-Lockean variant. Or it consists of beliefs, or sentences held true, in a common contemporary variant. The model here is the explicit, the formulated. Ideally, one could imagine making an inventory of what we know. Even though this would be impossible to complete, in one sense, because the possible entailments of what we believe are potentially endless, nevertheless we would always be dealing with explicit entailments of explicit elements.

3. In seeking to justify our beliefs, we can never go beyond/below these explicit, formulated elements, and in particular those, if any, which have the status of immediate givens.

4. The fourth strand is what we called above the dualist sorting, the mental-physical distinction. What continues here is the conceptual opposition, not the actual belief in a dualism. Many contemporaries scornfully reject the idea of souls or immaterial substances of any kind. The whole furniture of heaven and earth ultimately can be explained as matter. But in this they are operating within the same conceptual grid. First, that which they claim to be the universal basis of all phenomena is exactly the "physical" as it emerges out of the Cartesian revolution, that is, the material world no longer seen as the expression or manifestation of meaning or "Ideas," devoid of inner teleology, the realm of purely efficient causation. So the move to materialism accepts the sorting, but claims that only one term is really instantiated. But second, the "mental" has to remain a category for them, in that materialism is more a program than a theory; they have still to show that thinking, feeling, knowledge, action—all the phenomena in the range of mind or intelligence—can be explained in purely material terms. But to explain something you first have to pick it out; and they in fact pick it out in the basic terms of the dualist sorting, the "mental" as the realm of inner appearance, where to be is to be experienced. Hence the focus on sensation and raw feels and "qualia" in the whole reductive enterprise, which aims to convince us that in the end, these are "only" brain -states.

The dualist sorting: there are bodily, extended things; and then there are things which are not these, and so "mental," nonextended, perfectly non-physical; this comes with the mechanization of the world picture. We now have mental-physical as an obvious distinction. But there is also the problem of relating them—the "mind-body" problem. This is a very modern conception. We would have had trouble explaining this way of conceiving things to Plato, or Aristotle.

But even we, if we reflect a little, can see that this way of carving things up is not necessarily "obvious." Take "physical" desire, as against other, "higher," less physical desires. We can still make sense of this distinction, even though we may also want to reject the implicit hierarchy in the name of some humanist moral stance, affirming the value of sensual life. And then we can look backward, to the older topology of sense, imagination, intellect—*aisthesis, phantasia, nous*—which we mentioned above. This is quite different from the modern idea of the "mind" as a single "space," which we referred to above in connection with Descartes.

Herbert Feigl defined the distinction in these terms: the "mental" was defined by the "phenomenal," something we have direct access to by "acquaintance." "Acquaintance as such" means "the direct experience itself, as lived through, enjoyed, or suffered."[13]

The idea here is to take something which is only available from the first-person (singular) perspective, and consider it as a separate entity. So you don't have one entity, say, my life as it is unfolding, which is seen from different perspectives. But alongside the externally observable reality, we postulate something whose *esse* is *percipi*, to borrow Berkeley's expression. This is explained in terms of inner-outer structure, although the rationalizations of the inner reality are different. We can think of them as just "appearance" for modern materialism. But for Descartes and the first version of epistemology, we have here immaterial substance. That's why it's not available from outside.

The older, premodern ontologies didn't carve things up this way. What we think of as mind and body interpenetrate. For Plato and Aristotle, for instance, the things around us are shaped by Ideas, or Forms. Their

---

13. Herbert Feigl, *The "Mental" and the "Physical": The Essay and the Postscript* (Minneapolis: University of Minnesota Press, 1967).

models were partly living things, and partly artifacts. Purpose was every-where. But this was also true of the implicit ontologies of everyday life in premodern times, where people lived in what we can call, building on Weber's expression, an enchanted world. There one found things, like love potions for instance, which had causal powers which were defined in meaning terms . These were not conceived like a modern aphrodisiac, which may make you desire, but doesn't determine the ultimate human meaning of this desire. They were really love potions. King Marke forgives Tristan and Isolde because he sees that their transgression came about in the grip of this magic power.

Or think of a relic which cures; this is not like medicine, which works on a specific malady. Here you are cured of whatever ails you. Or take mel-ancholy, which was black bile. The idea was that mood and substance were one. "Modern" beliefs don't have this structure. We do know chemicals whose ingestion can induce depression. The depression is an effect, due to the way the drug impacts our body chemistry. We don't see the meaning as consubstantial with the drug itself.

We can think of the drug's effect as an invasion—something you can fight against. You may even get a sense of relief when you learn that you feel bad because of some chemical; because then it hasn't really touched you; you are not gloomy for some good reason; you can disengage from the mood. But in the old days, when you heard that you had black bile, then you knew you were in the grips of the real thing.[14]

Modern post-Cartesian dualism is not like Platonic dualism. Because for Plato, the lower is expressive of the higher. So we disengage from the lower by loving the higher through it. This is the movement of Eros, as described in the *Symposium*. But Descartes disengages from the bodily through objec-tifying it, seeing it as just dead, unexpressive stuff.

In fact, we can say that the founding move of the modern dualist sort-ing, and of the mechanization of the world picture, was this Cartesian kind of disengagement, which disinvests the world of objects around us of any meaning, be it the ordinary everyday meanings that things have for us as embodied agents—being available or out of reach, pressing on us or open,

---

14. This point has been discussed at further length in Charles Taylor, chap. 11 in *Sources of the Self* (Cambridge, MA: Harvard University Press, 1989).

attractive or repulsive, inviting or forbidden—or be it the intrinsic purposes defined by Ideas. Descartes wanted not only, following Galileo, to deny the older teleological view of nature, but strove for a more thoroughgoing objectification of the material, one which would include our own lived bodies as well. We had to step from the ordinary, embodied perspective, in which the felt heat was seen as in the object, and the pain as in the tooth, and grasp the process in the way an outside observer can, where certain experiences in the mind are caused by certain conditions in the physical world, say, the kinetic energy of molecules in the object, or the decay in the tooth.

That this is the step which generates clarity and distinctness in this domain of sensations and secondary properties is made evident by Descartes on a number of occasions. In one place, he says that "the ideas which I have of heat and cold contain so little clarity and distinctness" (*les idées que j'ay du froid & de la chaleur sont si peu claires & si peu distinctes*); in another, he says: "We know that pain and color and other sentiments are clearly and distinctly perceived when they are regarded merely as . . . thoughts" (*nous connoissons clairement et distinctement la douleur, la couleur et les autres sentimens, lors que nous les considerons simplement comme . . . des pensées*); in yet another, he speaks of "these sentiments and sense perceptions having been placed in me only to signify to my mind what things are beneficial or damaging for the composite of which the mind is a part" (*ces sentimens ou perceptions des sens n'ayant esté mises en moy que pour signifier à mon esprit quelles choses sont convenables ou nuisibles au composé dont il est partie, jusque là estant assez claires et assez distinctes*). In other words, grasped from outside, as body-to-mind causal connections with a survival function, these obscure experiences become clear.[15]

It is this dualist sorting, and the underlying disengagement from the embodied stance, which has been consecrated in the tradition as the proper "scientific" stance to things human. This is just as much, if not more, in evidence in the materialist ambition to explain all action and thinking in terms of matter disinvested of meaning, as it was in the original dualist perspective

---

15. Quotations respectively from *Meditations*, III, Adam and Tannery, IX-1, 34; *Principles*, I.68, Adam and Tannery, IX-2, 56; *Meditations*, VI, Adam and Tannery, IX-1, 66. See also Alan Gewirth's discussion in his "Clearness and Distinctness in Descartes," in *Descartes: A Collection of Critical Essays*, ed. William Doney (Garden City, NY: Doubleday 1967), 260n33.

of Descartes and Locke.[16] And it is reflected as well in the impoverished category of the "mental" as inner appearance, whether or not it is ultimately to be shown as "identical" to brain states.

This is the point behind the claim often made by critics of this mediational tradition, that modern reductive theories of the mind are essentially still "Cartesian," an accusation which protagonists of this reductivism perceive as wildly misplaced and unfair. Relevant here is the vogue in recent decades for accounts of thinking based on the idea that the brain operates in some respects like a digital computer. These were very popular for a number of decades, and have not really been fully replaced in the imagination of many thinkers in cognitive science.

The computer model exhibits all four of the continuing strands of the mediational tradition outlined above. (1) It speaks of the mind as receiving "inputs" from the environment, and producing "outputs." (2) Computations proceed on the basis of bits of clearly defined information, which get processed. The brain computes explicit bits of information. (3) The brain as a computer is a purely "syntactic engine"; its computations get their "reference" to the world through these "inputs." And (4) the account proceeds on the materialist basis that these mental operations are to be explained by the physical operations of the underlying engine, the brain. Mechanism and formalism, that is, being driven by formal procedures, which Descartes distributed between his two substances, body and mind, are now reunited in the body. But this is no mere external synthesis. Thinking by explicit formal rules consorts with mechanism, because both exclude the kind of not totally transparent intuitions that humans have as embodied, social, and cultural agents: knowing whether I can jump this

---

16. The aim of "scientific naturalism," as Jennifer Hornsby describes it, is to account for the actions, feelings, intentions, etc., of persons from the "objective, third-personal perspective" that natural scientists adopt. The underlying belief is that everything which is real must be intelligible from that perspective. Hornsby's argument is that many of the phenomena of personal life just disappear when we adopt this perspective. Against this pervasive current in modern thought, she proposes a "naïve" naturalism, which recognizes the difference between human and inanimate. See J. Hornsby, *Simple Mindedness* (Cambridge, MA: Harvard University Press, 1997), 4–5. We are very much in agreement with this position, even appreciating the irony of the title she gives to a thesis which is immensely more sophisticated than the knee-jerk scientism she opposes.

ditch, whether you are mad at me, that the atmosphere at the party has suddenly become tense.

Indeed, this connection underlay one of Turing's key intuitions, that a purely formal system must be operable by a machine, because then you know that none of these nontransparent intuitions are, unknown and unbidden, filling in the gaps in the reasoning. As Marvin Minsky put it: "If the procedure can be carried out by some very simple machine, so that there can be no question of or need for 'innovation' or 'intelligence', then we can be sure that the specification is complete, and that we have an 'effective procedure'."[17] This is what John Haugeland speaks of as the "automation principle: wherever the legal moves of a formal system are fully determined by algorithms, then that system can be automated."[18]

3

Now we're sure that many readers will not see the continuing force of these four strands: the "only through" structure (1), the explicitness of content (2), which one can't get beyond/below (3), and the dualist sorting (4), as at all surprising, let along worrying. Are not these the inevitable conclusions of common sense informed by modern science? What else can we think about these matters?

We are not surprised or perturbed by this reaction. What else do you expect when we're dealing with one of these deeply embedded pictures in Wittgenstein's sense, which "hold us captive" just because they seem so obvious, so unchallengeable, so without alternative?

But we can't leave things here, at a standoff, in which each side is unruffled by the claims of the other. And it is part of the aim of this book to try to take us beyond, and to make it convincing that there is a picture, and an inadequate one, which has dominated thinking for too long. We hope the further argument will help this project along. But at this point, perhaps it

17. See Marvin Minsky, *Computation: Finite and Infinite Machines* (Englewood Cliffs, NJ: Prentice Hall, 1967), 105.

18. See John Haugeland, *Artificial Intelligence: The Very Idea* (Cambridge, MA: Bradford/MIT Press, 1985), 82.

would help to loosen up some too-firm intuitions to point out that there are and have been alternatives to the picture defined by (1)–(4).

What is involved in an alternative? If the four elements define a mediational theory, an alternative view would have to be called a "contact theory." Where a mediation theory seeks knowledge as arising through some mediational element, so that we have contact with the real in knowledge only through some intermediary, depiction, or category, contact theories give an account of knowledge as our attaining unmediated contact with the reality known.

This sounds like what used to be called "naïve realism," pronounced in a condescending tone of voice; for of course, it appears terribly unsophisticated and prereflective to those who are into the mediational picture. But some rather sophisticated views in our philosophical tradition were contact theories. For instance, Plato's account of real knowledge, as against shadowy and evanescent opinion, in the *Republic*, turns on what reality one is in contact with, the really real and unchanging, or the ever-changing flux. He invokes the image of the eye of the soul, which either turns towards the dark side of the universe, focused only on the ever-moving and temporary copies, or swivels around to the side where light illuminates the eternal Ideas.[19] Here there is no hint of a mediating element; nothing separates us from reality. Real knowledge is a kind of unmediated contact.

Of course, we might protest that all this is metaphor, not real "theory." But then we might look at Aristotle, and the view of knowledge he presents in the *De Anima*. Here he says that actualized knowledge (*episteme*), is one with the object.[20] The idea seems to be that just as the real object is what it is because it is shaped by the Form (*eidos*) appropriate to its kind, so the intellect (*nous*) in its own very different way can come to be shaped by different *eidê*. In correct knowledge of an object, the *nous* comes to be shaped by the same *eidos* that forms the object. There is no question here of a copy or a depiction; there is one and only one *eidos* of any kind. When I see this animal and know it as a sheep, mind and object are one because they come together

19. At 518c–d of *The Republic*, Plato speaks of a "conversion," a "turning around" (*periagôgê*).

20. "Actual knowledge is identical with its object" (*to d' auto estin hê kat' energeian epistêmê tôi pragmati*). Book III, 430a20; and again at 431a1 in *De Anima*.

in being formed by the same *eidos*.[21] That is why it is *actualized* knowledge which forms becomes one with its object. If we can introduce an image here to make the underlying idea intuitively stronger, we can think of the Form as a kind of rhythm giving shape to both objects and intellects. Where there is knowledge, the self-same rhythm joins mind and thing. They become one in this single movement. There is unmediated contact.

So we broke down and had recourse to metaphor after all. This may say something about philosophical theorizing, rather than about our lack of theoretical capacity. But at least we hope to have shown that contact theories have been propounded in our philosophical tradition, and that they are not necessarily irremediably weird. But in the case of these two famous ancients, the understanding of contact very much depends on their ontology—in fact, on the theory of Forms, the idea that the reality around us is what it is in virtue of being shaped by Ideas. But once we have been through the Galilean revolution, and the mechanization of the world picture, even if we don't extend this to human thought and action, this older, cosmically embedded teleology can no longer appear plausible to us.

And so what in fact has emerged in modern philosophy is a new kind of contact theory, not dependent on the old teleology. This type of theory reached a high degree of self-clarity and articulation during the early twentieth century. Prominent among its framers were, for instance, Heidegger, Merleau-Ponty, and Wittgenstein. A basic move which gives rise to this theory is a reembedding of thought and knowledge in the bodily and social-cultural contexts in which it takes place. The attempt is to articulate the framework or context within which our explicit depictions of reality make sense, and to show how this is inseparable from our activity as the kind of embodied, social, and cultural beings we are. The contact here is not achieved on the level of Ideas, but is rather something primordial, something we never escape. It is the contact of living, active beings, whose life form involves acting in and on a world which also acts on them. These beings are at grips with a world and each other; this original contact provides the sense-making context for all their knowledge constructions, which, however

21. Later Aristotle says that "knowledge is the knowable and sensation is the sensible." This doesn't mean that the sensible and cognitive faculties are identical with the object as a material entity, "for the stone doesn't exist in the soul, but only the form of a stone" (431b22, 432a1). It is in the *eidos* that the mind and object come together.

much they are based on mediating depictions, rely for their meaning on this primordial and indissoluble involvement in the surrounding reality.

4

We want to move in Chapter 2 to expound certain aspects of this theory. But first, we'd like to lay out here a contrast in the logics of mediational and contact theories, because a failure to appreciate these differences has led to a great deal of cross-purposes, of uncomprehending talking past each other.

For contact theories, truth is self-authenticating. When you're there, you know you're there. But for the mediational variety, this can never be. A common approach here is to take knowledge to be justified, true belief. First there is belief: what I'm inclined to say; to rise to the level of knowledge, this has first to be true, say, to correspond to the way things are; then there have to be good grounds for holding the belief. The definition of good grounds focuses us on the search for marks or criteria.

There are two important features of justification here, which mark the difference with contact theories. One is that I am supposed to be able to account for my confidence that this belief is true in terms of a finite number of features which I can separate out, isolate, and take as criteria.

Now in many contexts in life, it doesn't seem intuitively obvious that this requirement is appropriate. I'm certain that we're now in 2014, that I'm in the Laurentians, that I'm trying to write some lectures on epistemology, and so on. If you ask me why I'm so sure, I can only splutter; I don't know what to say. Perhaps better put, I don't know where to start. There are too many things to say here. But this doesn't get to the heart of what seems queer. It's not just that there are a heap of independently identifiable signs. It's much more that there are considerations of a quite different order. These things belong to the background which is being taken as firm as we go about examining/questioning other things.

Wittgenstein in *On Certainty* mentions the kind of issue which would arise if someone asked whether the world hasn't started only five minutes ago.[22] There it is, as we experience it, with all that we take as signs of earlier

---

22. Wittgenstein starts an issue of this kind in *On Certainty*, para 84, and it then recurs periodically throughout the work.

ages, including our memory-beliefs and fossils in the rocks, but it nevertheless all came into being just a few minutes ago. When someone raises this
somewhat far-fetched supposition, and we reject it, does this mean that we
have always had a belief that the world stretches back into the mists of time?
Have we been proceeding on the "assumption" that the world goes way back?
This doesn't seem right. Rather we should say that a world stretching back
indefinitely operated as a kind of framework or context which made sense of
a great many questions we asked and explicit inquiries we engaged in, such as
the dating of these fossils, estimating the age of these mountains, explaining
certain features of the landscape by the hypothesis that there was once a sea
here, and the like. This framework wasn't an assumption, or a belief; it was
just taken, unquestioned, as the framework. Indeed, it never occurred to us
that we could question it in this way, until this strange suggestion was made.

Does this mean that we weren't careful enough, that we hadn't got down
to the real rock-bottom reasons for our beliefs? So that we should reconstruct our knowledge, now with the additional premise that the world didn't
start just five minutes ago? But Wittgenstein's point is that this kind of foundational ambition is vain. We are always and inevitably thinking within such
taken-as-there frameworks. Otherwise put, the number of things which an
eccentric, philosophical mind could raise questions about is indefinite, endless. We would never get to the bottom. In the nature of things, some or
other such framework will always be there, making sense of what we do.
Frameworks shift, when we learn to problematize certain things, but as a
class they are inescapable. In particular, where and when we are form part of
the framework of our lives, in relation to which we go about the things we're
doing, including the things we question and argue about.

By contrast, the mediational approach seems to want to take each belief
as though it were there on its own, standing alone, frameworkless. That is
why it makes sense to think of justification purely in terms of criteria. Why
do this? Because it seems right, prudent. Because we have been wrong, the
framework has often turned out to be unreliable, to have error built into
it. For instance, the original macro-time-framework of our civilization was
contained within the Bible story, understood not "literally," because this issue didn't arise in its present form until modern times, but understood in
the way similar legends have usually been understood. The story gives us the
train of important events since the beginning. Then later, in the eighteenth
century and after, there arose the sense of the "dark abyss of time." Within

this later framework, the hypothesis of a recent genesis replete with signs of longer existence arises as a "literalist" response, intended to reassert biblical authority.

So there have been corrections; and where they have been made, we usually have good reasons for them. So what's wrong with saying that we always need reasons, even when we're unaware that we are believing certain things without proper reasons? Doesn't accepting the framework uncritically amount to a kind of dogmatism, a claim that we could never be wrong? Well no, because there are scenarios of error and correction, as we just saw with our time framework. And there are other more banal, recognized predicaments: we have been conned, drugged, manipulated. Various error stories can be proposed to challenge our position. If a supposition of this kind is raised, we might have to check things out, in relation to this story. But the response of the contact theorist is that this (exceptional) case would also have to be handled in the context of our general grasp on our world.

The point is, that unless we can make sense of a foundationalist justification which goes right down to unchallengeable elements, uninterpreted impressions, or "simple ideas," we will always be thinking within frameworks which are vulnerable to potential challenges and revisions. Our confidence in these at any one time reflects our sense that while operating within them we are in contact with reality. This confidence may (we can say, almost certainly will) turn out to be misplaced in some as-yet-unpredictable respects. But never totally, because we will only be able to cope with these errors within an amended framework. Within the frameworks, we of course cope with issues by giving reasons, invoking criteria. We frame representations about which we ask whether they really apply. We treat our beliefs, theories, as over against reality, to be related to it. But all this goes on within a larger context of presumed contact with reality. The presumption can be erroneous, but never totally. That is the aspect which contact theories grasp and mediational accounts lose sight of.

In virtue of our framework, certain suppositions will appear frivolous, even absurd; like the "five minutes ago" story above. Perhaps we're wrong here; perhaps the far-out innovators are onto something? This can happen; but it certainly isn't always so. Think of the strained, obsessively suspicious arguments of contemporary Holocaust deniers.

The second feature differentiating the understandings of justification concerns how we inhabit time. Our general sense of things, where/when we are, what we're about, is path dependent. I know I'm here, in the Laurentians, because I've come here. Our grasp of things is not only couched in a timeless or an instantaneous present. We also have perfect-tensed understandings. We are here, because we have made our way here; "we are come," as older usage has it.

The grasp on things of temporal beings is not couched in a series of present-tensed claims, that things are thus and so, for which some of the criterial signs are memories, which purport to be of past events, we might say aorist events. In Benveniste's famous discussion, the French perfect (*le passé composé*) relates the events described to the speaker's situation, whereas the aorist (*le passé simple*) leaves this relation indeterminate.[23] The point we are making here is that there are certain aspects of our grasp on reality which can only properly be couched in perfect-tensed statements. Like knowing you're here.

This is part of what underlies the self-authenticating nature of the truth on the contact view. You know because you're there. This is inseparable from having come there. We have what we could call a transitional grasp on reality. We'll get to this later, in connection with the modes of argument available when we confront different outlooks. But let's take the banal case of dreaming. We wake up, and it is this which assures us that we are really there, in contact with reality. A similar point was made by Plato in relation to the dialectic. You know you're there—in contact with the really real—because you've climbed there out of error.

The convincing power of the skeptical argument connected with dreaming, as we see in Descartes' first *Meditation*, comes from its placing us within the dream. At that moment, we can be, indeed usually are, fooled. But in our perfect-tensed awareness of having awakened, there is no further question.

But what about the supposition that life itself is dreamlike? Life is a dream (*La vida es sueño*), as Calderòn would have it? Perhaps this is so, but only in relation to a deeper awakening; and we can only know this is so in that awakening.

The mediational construal of the dream predicament, as with Descartes, sees my situation as my having been confronted with a convincing appearance, which now seems unreal. But the perfect-tensed awareness is clear that

23. Émile Benveniste, *Problèmes de Linguistique générale*, vol. 1 (Paris: Gallimard, 1966), chap. 19.

this was not convincing; things were wandering all over the place. Dreams are notoriously wayward and fantastic once one tries to describe them on waking. Only my critical distance from this was zero, or very small. The same is true of many hallucinations.

These two points belong together. Our particulate awarenesses, our grasp on particular things, are embedded in a more general framework take, which gives them their sense. This take is holistic: you can't break it down into a heap of particulate grasps; and—what is the same thing from another side—it is inescapable: all particulate grasps suppose it, lean on it. Second, this holistic take has temporal depth. This is the point explored by Heidegger with the notion of *Zeitlichkeit*.

The central issue between the two views concerns the framework. Of course, contact theorists agree that certain questions can be treated by invoking criteria—the ones raised within the framework. But not all can be. Mediational theories tend to make this treatment everywhere applicable. At the heart of the mediational theory is an invocation of good method, and its universal applicability. It assumes the stance of an inquiring mind, distrustful of possible easy illusions. Or it adopts a forensic style, like a good trial lawyer. Don't just accept the overall picture you're being offered; break things down. What did you really see, Mr. Jones? Please tell us exactly. No inferences, please.

This stance got much plausibility from the awareness, inseparable from the Galilean revolution, of the unreliability of the common sense, "natural" take on things. The sun does indeed seem to "go down"; the cart seems to stop as soon as you leave off pushing it. But we know that things happen very differently. The refusal of any limits to this good forensic method is foundationalism. That's what Descartes and Locke offer us. You start from the purely given, and then build up by responsible inferences. This classical epistemology in fact ontologized good method. The right way to deal with puzzles and build a trustworthy body of knowledge is to break the issue down into subquestions, identify the chains of inference, dig down to an inference-free starting point, and then build by a reliable procedure. Once this comes to seem the all-purpose nostrum for thinking, then one has an overwhelming motivation to believe that that is how the mind actually works in taking in the world. Because if not, one has to draw the devastating conclusion that the only reliable method is inapplicable in the most important context of all, where we build our knowledge of the world. So epistemology dictates ontology. Foundationalism defines how the mind in fact functions. Only it can do it sloppily, without attention, following external authority; or it can do it carefully, self-scrutinizingly, self-responsibly.

We can see how cross-purposes can easily arise. For the imagination nourished by this mediational tradition, it seems that we can normally give reasons for our beliefs, find criteria which show them to be right. Where this is not the case, it is because we have got to rock bottom, to the purely given, prior to all interpretation. This purely given is the "incorrigible"; we can doubt it, but we can't improve on it, amend it, or check it. So when contact theorists talk of things we know because we're there, things we grasp without identifiable criteria, it naturally appears as though they're talking about matters which are "incorrigible." But this, as we saw above, is not the case. Frameworks can be challenged, and amended. But something subject to amendment, which is nevertheless known without criteria, doesn't make sense on a foundationalist understanding; and so we often end up talking past each other.

The irony is that this carefully constructed foundationalist theory ended up producing another, unreflective *Bild*, a new "common sense," which needs to be challenged. This is what we shall attempt to do in Chapter 2.

5

Some of the motivation for the mediational theory was implicit in the previous paragraphs. It reflects a stance of critical awareness, unwilling simply to take things on authority, or to accept the first-off, easiest, most convenient interpretation. It calls for a self-responsible verification in reason of the beliefs that are too often taken over unthinkingly. But this is not only an epistemic stance; it is part of a broader ideal, that of freedom and personal responsibility, which determines a way of being in the world in general, and not just a way of practicing science.

And indeed, we are aware that this ethic of personal responsibility has been a key component of Western modernity. It is central to the Reformed spiritualities, on both the Protestant and the Catholic side, and then it takes on secularized forms, and comes to expression in the ideals of reason and autonomy, and the political norms of self-government. In fact, "critical" has become a keyword of approbation; as a self-description it counts as an endorsement of one's stance.

At a deeper level, the stance of disengagement has also benefitted from a powerful ethical charge. It is strongly valued insofar as it is seen as inseparable from freedom, responsibility, and the self-transparency which we gain by reflection on our own thinking. But the objectification of the world which it achieves is also the condition of a certain control over it. As long as we see ourselves in a cosmos which manifests certain moral and spiritual meanings, our attitudes are or ought to be determined by the significances which are inherent in things. But once we come to see the world as mechanism, a domain of efficient causation, but without inherent purpose, then we are free to treat it as a neutral field where our main concern is how to affect our own purposes. Instrumental reason becomes the only appropriate category, and knowledge can be seen as the basis of power.

At a deeper level again, disengagement is not only a source of power; it also is the instrument of disenchantment. The world ceases to be the locus of spirits and magic forces. One of the age-old primordial sources of fear and awe in human life, which so easily can be renewed in the infancy of each one of us, is negated and dried up. There is a sense of invulnerability, in relation to the immemorial sense of being at the mercy of spirits and forces—but also the intuition that this invulnerability was hard won. It required effort, and also courage, to face down the primordial fears, and abandon the sense of comfort in our niche that a meaningful cosmos offers. And this generates a feeling of pride.

Modern disengaged agency continuously generates a discourse of self-congratulation, lauding the courage and effort that produced the free, critical agent. Typical is Ernest Jones's depiction of Freud as a hero of modernity in succession to Copernicus and Darwin. Each one of these was willing to abandon the self-flattering and comforting picture of a meaningful world in which we had pride of place, be it the world at the center of the cosmos, humans as quite different from animals, or the human mind as riding high beyond bodily feeling, in order to face the discomforting, even anguishing truth.

So a lot more is going for mediational epistemology, beyond its supposed efficacy in producing valid and reliable beliefs. Powerful ideals and a sense of dignity attach to this way of being, and these help to make it seem unchallengeable and devoid of a worthy alternative. But in order to understand the attempts to deconstruct the mediational view, we should also note that the disengaged stance has generated forceful reactions which have been gathering strength since the Romantic period. The sense has grown that this stance cuts us off from the world, from nature, from society, even from our own emotional nature. We are divided beings needing to be healed. The objective instrumental stance towards nature makes communion with it, or a sense of inclusion in it, impossible. Self-responsibility pushes us back to the first-person singular, makes us give primacy to the monological over the dialogical.

All of these complaints, right or wrong, have helped feed the challenge to the mediational view. The battle between the two construals, mediational and contact, is far from being a bloodless debate over scientific method. It is deeply involved in the contrary ethical and metaphysical passions of the modern age.

CHAPTER TWO

Escaping the Picture

OF COURSE, to be convinced that the mediational view is a "picture" in Wittgenstein's sense, and a distorting one, one has to follow the arguments which have "deconstructed" it. If the battle in our culture within which the deconstruction takes place is at least two hundred years old, as we claimed at the end of Chapter 1, then the process of refutation, and the emergence of the new, modern contact view has also been in process for some time.

Now there are two basic axes of refutation. We said above that the erroneous picture understands knowledge as the (correct) inner representation of outer reality. (1) One line of refutation consists in showing that our grasp of the world cannot be entirely representational; that is, it certainly involves representations, but these are not the whole story, not even the crucial part of the story. (2) But according to the dominant picture, derived originally from Descartes, this inner picture is in the individual mind. Knowledge, properly understood, not only consists of representations, but is also lodged primarily within individual minds. These minds may exchange, and there may be some form of social pooling, as with libraries, encyclopedias, and Internet sites, but this shared knowledge is ultimately a compound of the knowings of individuals. Building valid knowledge out of the original input is primarily a monological process. A second line of refutation targets this monological thesis. Its aim is to show that our gasp of the world is first of all shared, and then only secondarily imparted to each one of us, as we are inducted into the language and culture of our society. Of course, we then can make additions and modifications as individuals, but these affect what is originally a common store which each of us receives from outside.

Refutation on line (1) takes after the primacy of representation; the attack on line (2) targets *individual* representation, the primacy of the monological.

We start off in the following chapters following line (1). In a sense, the earliest move on this line goes back to Kant, even though in crucial ways he remained within the mediational view. Hegel represents another crucial stage; but it wasn't until the first half of the twentieth century that the alternative approach reached a full articulation.

1

There are many strands to this first refutation/deconstruction, as we might expect. One attacks the Myth of the Given, the idea that our knowledge grounds in the reception of preinterpreted data. This seems to make experience problematic. We reason, argue, make inferences, and arrive at an understanding of the world. But our framework understanding, which most of these theories try to retain, is that we also learn from the world; we take things in, come to know things, on the basis of which we reason. It was this dual source of our knowledge which mediational epistemologies were meant to capture in their basic structure: receptivity produces the basic elements of input, and then reasoning processes these into science.

But the very boundary set up by the mediational element seemed to make it hard to conceive how these two sources could work together. What seemed like obvious solutions just enhanced another set of problems, those connected with skepticism and nonrealism, which we will discuss below. These solutions would amount to the idea that receptivity is to be understood in purely causal terms, that it just delivers certain results which we can't get behind; and reason then does what it can to make sense of these.

But beyond this, the very idea of a boundary can be made to seem highly problematic. Critical reasoning is something we do, an activity, in the realm of spontaneity and freedom. But, as far as knowledge of the world is concerned, it is meant to be responsive to the way things are. Spontaneity has to be merged somehow with receptivity. But it is hard to see how this can be, if we conceive of spontaneity as a kind of limitless freedom, which at the point of contact has to hit a world under adamantine, post-Galilean "laws of nature." The schizophrenic nature of boundary events, inexplicably partaking of both nature and freedom, is an inevitable consequence of this way of seeing things.

And so the very idea of a boundary event, between a realm of causes and a realm of reasons, begins to seem contradictory. This event would have to be in a sense amphibious, belonging to both; and yet are their natures not contradictory? On the one hand an object, or a factual state of affairs, the causal upshot in our receptors of outside stimulation; on the other hand certain *claims*, to the effect that so-and-so, which could figure as reasons to adopt some broader view or other. This is the consideration which has led some philosophers to denounce the Myth of the (purely) Given, the brute, uninterpreted fact.[1]

The problem has been to account for experience, in the sense of a taking in of information from the world. In one way we have to receive this information; we are the passive party. In another, we have to know how to "grasp" it; we are active. How do these two combine?

This has been the notorious problem of the tradition of modern philosophy which has been defined by modern epistemology. In certain well-known classical writers, the absence of any plausible theory of experience was patent. Leibniz in the end denied it altogether, and saw a picture of the world as present in its entirety within the monad. Hume seemed to go to the other extreme, and allow that all our knowledge comes to us through experience—hence the vaunted title "empiricist"; but this was at the cost of denying the active dimension altogether, so that the deliverances of experience were unconnected bits of information, and what seems to ordinary people as the undeniable connections were denounced as projections of the mind. Even the self disappears in this caricatural passivism.

1. See John McDowell, *Mind and World* (Cambridge, MA: Harvard University Press, 1993), lecture 1.

Kant notoriously tried to unite Hume and Leibniz. At least he saw the problem, how to combine spontaneity and receptivity. But he was still too caught up in the mediationalist structure to propound a believable solution.[2]

2

But the most influential strand in the twentieth century was what we will call the "metacritical" one.[3] The idea of a metacritique here is, as the name suggests, to inquire into the basis of first-order critical theory. This latter claims to reflect on the conditions of our everyday or scientific knowledge claims, and to upset the ordinary precritical view we have of them. The metacritique reflects in turn on the conditions of our making this kind of critique.

But the search for conditions takes place in a different dimension, as yet unexplored by the founders of the mediational tradition—though not neglected by Kant: this is what makes him the hinge figure. The attempt is to explore the context which has to be taken as given if we are to make sense of the critical enterprise, and beyond this of our experience of the world as such. Just what is the understanding of mind-in-world which would make sense of the suppositions of mediational theory? And is this consistent with the understanding which makes sense of experience as we actually live it?

We've already been engaged in developing an answer to the first question in Chapter 1, when we tried to articulate the Cartesian view of mind-in-world, in showing the importance of the dualist sorting, for instance. Now even the answer to this first question can be very unsettling for the mediational approach. Since this was developed in the first instance with foundationalist intent, the aim being to find a solid basis for knowledge by digging down to the purely given which we can't see behind, to be told that the enterprise depends on adopting a particular view of mind-in-world, to

2. We have drawn on the extremely insightful work of Samuel Todes, whose doctoral dissertation was published, many years after it was written, as *Body and World* (Cambridge, MA: MIT Press, 2001).

3. We take our cue here from a work by Hamann, *The Metacritique of Pure Reason*, which comments on Kant. Also relevant is a book by Herder, *Understanding and Experience: A Metacritique of the Critique of Pure Reason*.

which there are after all alternatives, is utterly devastating. For if the argument can only proceed by our taking on board one among other possible interpretations of mind-in-world, then the claim to have reached the foundation is voided—unless this interpretation can in turn be solidly grounded.

This argumentative move, where one puts foundationalism in contradiction with itself, is made to good effect by Hegel in the introduction to *The Phenomenology of Spirit*.[4] What this shows is what we wanted to claim above, that foundationalism can only proceed if one is in the grips of a *Bild* in Wittgenstein's sense, an unreflected embedding in one construal which is felt to be the only possible one, hence beyond all question.

But even in this introduction, Hegel is concerned with more than this pragmatic refutation. He wants to go on to explore the second question: What are the conditions which make sense of our experience of the world? He sees these as being defined in a series of negative moves whereby in each case we show the inadequacy of an earlier construal and amend it accordingly. The path towards an adequate construal is therefore defined as a dialectical movement, and the notion "experience" itself is given a richer sense, designating these moments of critical transition.

It is this second, dialectical form of argument that we want to follow here, where in each case we can show that a theory of knowledge violates the background conditions which would have to hold for it to be valid. Hegel turns this kind of argument against Kant, but ironically the mode of argument he draws on was itself inaugurated by Kant.

We could designate this as the foundational move in the search for the sense-making conditions of experience; and thus we see it deployed to great effect by Kant himself in the transcendental deduction. He inaugurates the line of argument that has been continued by the major "deconstructors" of the disengaged picture. This way of arguing, as we said above, undermines the picture by bringing out the background we need for the operations described in the picture to make sense, whereby it becomes clear that this background can't fit within the limits that the disengaged view prescribes. Once understood against its background, the account shows itself to be untenable.

---

4. G. W. F. Hegel, "Introduction," *Die Phänomenologie des Geistes* (Hamburg: Meiner Verlag, 1988). Hegel points out that the main epistemological tradition he is attacking supposes one or other picture of mind-in-world: either the mind can grasp reality through certain instruments, or reality comes to it through a "medium."

Kant didn't carry this argument as far as his twentieth-century successors. But he did manage to upset one of the crucial features of the mediational model, at least in an earlier variant. The arguments of the transcendental deduction can be seen in a number of different lights. But one way to take them is as a final laying to rest of a certain atomism of the input which had been espoused by empiricism. As this came to Kant through Hume, it seemed to be suggesting that the original level of knowledge of reality (whatever that turned out to be) came in particulate bits, individual "impressions." This level of information could be isolated from a later stage in which these bits were connected together, for example, in beliefs about cause-effect relations. We find ourselves forming such beliefs, but we can by taking a stance of reflexive scrutiny (which we saw above is fundamental to modern epistemology) separate the basic level from these too-hasty conclusions we leap to. This analysis allegedly reveals, for instance, that nothing in the phenomenal field corresponds to the necessary connection we too easily interpolate between "cause" and "effect."[5]

Kant undercuts this whole way of thinking by showing that it supposes, for each particulate impression, that it is being taken as a bit of potential information. It purports to be about something. The primitive distinction recognized by empiricists between impressions of sensation and those of reflection amounts to an acknowledgement of this. The buzzing in my head is discriminated from the noise I hear from the neighboring woods, in that the first is a component of how I feel, and the second seems to tell me something about what's happening out there. So even a particulate "sensation," really to be sensation (in the empiricist sense, that is, as opposed to reflection), has to have this dimension of "aboutness." This will later be called "intentionality," but Kant speaks of the necessary relation to an object of knowledge. "Now we find that our thought of the relation of all knowledge to its object carries with it an element of necessity" (*Wir finden aber, dass unser Gedanke von der Beziehung aller Erkenntniss auf ihren Gegenstand etwas von Notwendigkeit bei sich führe*).[6]

With this point secured, Kant argues that this relationship to an object would be impossible if we really were to take the impression as an utterly

5. David Hume, Section VII, *An Enquiry Concerning Human Understanding*. See *Enquiries* by David Hume, ed. L.A. Selby-Bigge (Oxford University Press 1902), 60–79.

6. Kant, *Kritik der reinen Vernunft*, A104. *Critique of Pure Reason*, trans. Norman Kemp Smith, A104 (London: Macmillan, 1929), 134.

isolated content, without any link to others. To see it as about something is to place it somewhere, at the minimum out in the world, as against in me, to give it a location in a world which, while it is in many respects indeterminate and unknown for me, cannot be wholly so. The unity of this world is presupposed by anything which could present itself as a particulate bit of *information*, and so whatever we mean by such a particulate bit, it couldn't be utterly without relation to all others. The background condition for this favorite supposition of empiricist philosophy, the simple impression, forbids us giving it the radical sense which Hume seemed to propose for it. To attempt to violate this background condition is to fall into incoherence. Really to succeed in breaking all links between individual impressions would be to lose all sense of awareness of anything. "These perceptions would not then belong to any experience, consequently would be without an object, merely a blind play of representations, less even than a dream" (*Diese [sc. Wahrnehmungen] würden aber alsdann auch zu keiner Erfahrung gehören, folglich ohne Objekt und nichts als ein blindes Spiel der Vorstellungen, d.i. weniger als ein Traum sein*).[7]

The transcendental deduction, and related arguments in the *Critique of Pure Reason*, can be seen as a turning point in modern philosophy. With hindsight, we can see them as the first attempt to articulate the background that the modern disengaged picture itself requires for the operations it described to be intelligible, and to use this articulation to undermine the picture. Once one goes through this transition, the whole philosophical landscape changes, because the issue of background understanding is out in the open. A crucial feature of the reified views which arise from ontologizing the canonical procedures of modern epistemology is that they make this issue invisible. The conditions of intelligibility are built into the elements and processes of the mind as internal properties. The isolated impression *is* intelligibly information on its own, just as the house is red or the table is square. It has all the particulate, separable existence of an external object. Locke treats simple ideas as analogous to the materials we use for building.[8] This outlook forgets that for something to be intelligibly X is for it to *count as* intelligibly X, and that there are always contextual conditions for anything to count as something.

7. Ibid., A112.
8. Locke, *Essay Concerning Human Understanding*, 2.2.2.

In its original Kantian form, this revolution sweeps away the atomism of modern epistemology. In this respect, he is followed by all those who have come after. In a sense the very move which dereifies our account of the knowing agent has an inherently holistic bent. What was formerly built into the elements is now attributed to the background which they all share.

Heidegger and Wittgenstein follow this pioneering Kantian form of argument. In *Sein und Zeit*, Heidegger argues that things are disclosed first as part of a world, that is, as the correlates of concernful involvement, and within a whole of such involvements. This undercuts certain basic features of the disengaged picture. First, following Kant, the atomism of input is denied by the notion of a whole of involvements. But it also undercuts another basic feature of the classical picture: that the primary input is neutral, and is only at a later stage attributed some meaning by the agent. This idea is negated by the basic thesis that things are first disclosed in a world as ready-to-hand (*zuhanden*). To think of this character as something we project onto things which are first perceived neutrally is to make a fundamental mistake.[9]

Heidegger's discussion in *Sein und Zeit* is sometimes taken by unsympathetic readers to be an interesting description of everyday existence which has no relevance to the philosophical issues of ontology he claims to be discussing. So we usually treat things as tools or obstacles, in their relevance to our activities—what does this show about the priority of neutral information? Of course, we aren't *aware* of things most of the time as neutral objects, but this doesn't show that the disengaged account isn't right. Our ordinary everyday consciousness must itself be seen as a construct. We mustn't make the pre-Galilean mistake of thinking that things are as they appear, even

---

9. "The kind of Being which belongs to these entities is readiness-to-hand. But this characteristic is not to be understood as merely a way of taking them, as if we were talking such 'aspects' into the 'entities' which we proximally encounter, or as if some world-stuff which is proximally present-at-hand in itself were 'given subjective coloring' in this way." Heidegger, *Being and Time*, trans. John Macquarrie and Edward Robinson (Oxford: Blackwell Ltd, 1967), 101. (*Die Seinsart dieses Seienden ist die Zuhandenheit. Sie darf jedoch nicht als blosser Auffassungscharakter verstanden werden, als würden dem zunächst begegnenden "Seienden" solche "Aspekte" aufgeredet, als würde ein zunächst an sich vorhandener Weltstoff in dieser Weise "subjektiv gefärbt".* Heidegger, *Sein und Zeit* [Tübingen: Niemeyer Verlag, 1967], 71.)

in matters of the mind. So runs a common complaint by supporters of the disengaged view against "phenomenology."

But Heidegger's intention is plainly other than just reminding us of what it's like to live in the world at an everyday level. The argument has the same purport as Kant's and could be invoked like his as an answer to the challenge we have just given voice to. The aim is to show that grasping things as neutral objects is one of our possibilities only against the background of a way of being in the world in which things are disclosed as ready-to-hand. Grasping things neutrally requires modifying our stance to them, which primitively has to be one of involvement. Heidegger is arguing like Kant that the comportment to things described in the disengaged view requires for its intelligibility to be situated within an enframing and continuing stance to the world which is antithetical to it, hence that this comportment couldn't be original and fundamental. The very condition of its possibility forbids us giving this neutralizing stance the paradigmatic and basic place in our lives that the disengaged picture supposes.

This argument about the conditions of possibility, the conditions of intelligibly realizing the stance, is carried in Heidegger's use of the term *ursprünglich*. It means not just "prior in time," but something stronger. Our *ursprünglich* stance comes before but also as a condition of what follows and modifies it. It is also carried in his repeated use of the phrase *zunächst und zumeist*. Once again this sounds deceptively weak. It is applied to a way of being that is not just there earlier and more frequently, but also provides the background for what is not it.

Heidegger's point can easily be misunderstood here. To say that we come to understand our world in the neutral terms of disengaged description or science only after we have already come to live in it as the locus of significances, is not to say that we have to define the concepts of neutral description in terms of the concepts of significance, the present-at-hand in terms of the ready-to-hand.

Let's look at the different ways in which a word can be intelligible for us, and/or in which things show up. For instance, things can show up in their significance for our action, as "affordances" in Gibson's phrase: this environment hems us in, that allows us to move; another one frustrates us, another one again facilitates what we want to do. Or things can show up as attractive or repulsive, pleasant or grating, soothing or anxiety arousing. These are all examples of things becoming intelligible in their meaning or significance for us.

But there are also ways in which things show up in a neutral mode, not in their significance for us, but as they appear to a disengaged agent, who is concerned just to make a neutral portrait of reality. This is the kind of way of making things intelligible which is central to and definitive of "science," particularly natural science.

Now there may be a certain order among these modes of intelligibility. Indeed, there can be more than one kind of order. One is a necessary sequence in the genesis of modes. It seems clear from the work of Heidegger and Merleau-Ponty that the "engaged" mode, in which things show up in their meanings for us, has to precede the disengaged one. Students of ontogenesis have argued that young children, for instance, who are just beginning to speak, can only learn new concepts in a context where the objects concerned have emotional significance for them.[10] Children suffering from autism, for whom the context of shared emotive reaction cannot be easily created, have greater difficulty in generalizing the concept and do so later than normal children. The very rituals in which children learn their first words are moments of communion, of the kind of shared attention which is intensely desired and sought by children, and without which they cannot flourish.

Again, children learn to discriminate weights in terms of difficulty and ease of lifting, before they learn the language of grams and kilos.

But it is clear that this necessary order of intelligibility has nothing to do with logical dependency, the way that grasping one concept requires that you grasp another. You can't grasp "bachelor" without some understanding of the institution of marriage, or you can't understand what "inflation" is without understanding what role prices play in our lives. Thus the fact that the engaged mode must be prior to the disengaged, which is a necessary sequencing in ontogenesis, because you can't get to the later stage except through the mastery of the earlier one, says nothing about the logical conditions for grasping the disengaged language of science. In contrast

10. Stanley Greenspan and Stuart Shanker, *The First Idea: How Symbols, Language, and Intelligence Evolved from Our Early Primate Ancestors to Modern Humans* (Cambridge, MA: DaCapo Press, 2004).

to the relation of bachelors to marriage and inflation to prices, a term like "weighs 10 kilos" is in no way related to "is too heavy" as a condition of its intelligibility.

Heidegger and Merleau-Ponty not only show that the engaged stance is unavoidably prior to the disengaged one genetically, but they also show that it remains an indispensable part of our lives. We never "grow out of" this way of making things show up, which remains unavoidable in our everyday moving around the world and coping with things. As we drive around the city, we see that we can slip in to the right of that slow car, and we can make that crossing before the oncoming truck smashes us; the spaces here are grasped in their "affordances." The engaged mode is, to recur to Heidegger's term above, the one we are in *zunächst und zumeist*, we might say "firstly and mostly," but its affordances are not part of what makes the language of disengaged science intelligible.

Now to return to our reprise of Kant's trailblazing argument in the twentieth century, Wittgenstein's way of proceeding in the *Philosophical Investigations* is even more obviously in line with the original. In a sense, he does for an atomism of meaning what Kant did for an atomism of information input. His target is a theory of language and meaning which, although he finds its paradigm statement in Augustine, was also espoused and developed by thinkers of the disengaged view. The atomism of meaning consisted in the view that a word was given meaning by being linked to an object in a relation of "naming" or "signifying." Not only is there a parallel here to the atomism of input of post-Cartesian epistemology, but the two were interwoven in the classical statements of this theory of the mind. Locke argues that a word gets its meaning not by signifying the object directly, but rather by signifying the idea in the mind which represents this object.[11] This amendment to the Augustinian theory is what opens the way to the supposition that each person might speak a different language, since different inner ideas might correspond in each person's mind to some public object which is being named. A quite private language, in which words mean things for me that no one else can know, now seems a distinct possibility, a skeptical threat not to be easily conjured. It is against this "modernized" form of the theory that Wittgenstein's array of arguments is largely deployed.

11. Locke, *An Essay Concerning Human Understanding*, 3.2.2.

The atomism of meaning turns out to be untenable for exactly the same reason as Kant demonstrated for the atomism of input. Its proponents suppose that a word can be given meaning in some ceremony of naming, or that its meaning can be imparted by pointing to the object it names. A good part of Wittgenstein's argument in the *Philosophical Investigations* consists in showing that the condition of this kind of "ostensive definition" working is that the learner understands a great deal about the workings of language, and the place of this particular word in it. The "grammar" of the relevant part of the language is presupposed, because this "shews the post [or position] where the new word is stationed" (*zeigt den Posten an, an den das neue Wort gestellt wird*).[12] Naming something seems like a primitive, self-sufficient operation, but when one takes it as such, "one forgets that a great deal of stage setting in the language is presupposed if the mere act of naming is to make sense" (*so vergisst man, dass schon viel in der Sprache vorbereitet sein muss, damit das blosse Benennen einen Sinn hat*).[13]

Wittgenstein talks explicitly in this last remark about the conditions of intelligibility. The idea that the meaning of a word just consists in its relation to the object it names, a conception which is by its nature atomistic, comes to grief on the realization that each such relation draws on a background understanding and doesn't make sense without it. But this understanding concerns not individual words, but the language games in which they figure, and eventually the whole form of life in which these games have sense. The Augustinian theory does come close to modeling bits of our understanding of language. But when we see the conditions of intelligibility of these bits, we are forced to abandon it as a model for language understanding in general. The theory was born of a reifying move. It built this background understanding into the individual word-thing relations and made them self-sufficient. The liberating step comes when one sees that they need a background and that one can explore this in all its richness and variety.

The theory supposes this whole background understanding, which we only acquire when we learn language, as already built in to the first word-thing relation we learn. This is the kind of position we're in when we learn a *second* language. We already know what it is for a word to have a place in the

12. Wittgenstein, *Investigations*, para 257.
13. Ibid.

whole, and usually have a sense of what the place is of the word they're now trying to teach us. The error is to read this condition back into the acquisition of our original language. "And now . . . we can say: Augustine describes the learning of human language as if the child came into a strange country and did not understand the language of the country; that is, as if it already had a language, only not this one" (*Und nun können wir . . . sagen: Augustinus beschreibe das Lernen der menschlichen Sprache so, als käme das Kind in ein fremdes Land und verstehe die Sprache des Landes nicht; das heisst: so als habe es bereits eine Sprache, nur nicht diese*).[14]

More recently, Robert Brandom has drawn on these different formulations of holism, and related them to the Fregean tradition, to produce a profound and far-reaching reformulation of epistemology and the philosophy of language.

He proposes to move from a theory which makes *representation* the fundamental concept to one which gives *inference* this central place. Representational theories follow the classical mold of the mediational tradition we have been sketching. They suppose that we can identify particular states of representation, through which we grasp particulate contents, which we then combine to produce an overall view of things.

By contrast, to make inference basic supposes a certain holism. Acquiring a new piece of information enables new inferences, because it enters into and reconfigures an already operative overall grasp of things. When I learn that a tiger is loose in the park, I know as well that I'd better not go there, that Aunt Mabel will be startled or worse on her way back from the hairdresser, that the zoo authorities are even more incompetent than I previously thought, that the mayor definitely has to be booted out at the next election for appointing his dense and feckless brother-in-law as the chair of the zoo committee, and so forth.

In other words, there is no such thing as an absolutely isolated bit of information, unlinked by inferences, fore and aft.[15]

14. Ibid., para 32.

15. Robert B. Brandom, *Making It Explicit: Reasoning, Representing, and Discursive Commitment* (Cambridge, MA: Harvard University Press, 1994), especially chap. 2; *Articulating Reasons: An Introduction to Inferentialism* (Cambridge, MA: Harvard University Press, 2000), especially introduction and chap. 1; *Tales of the Mighty Dead: Historical Essays in the Metaphysics of Intentionality* (Cambridge, MA: Harvard University Press, 2002).

3

The major deconstructions of mediationalism took place in the twentieth century along this line of articulating the sense-making conditions of experience. It was in the course of this that the mediational picture emerged as a distortion, at the same time that an alternative contact theory was being elaborated. A certain kind of holism is essential to this alternative view. From the standpoint of this alternative, the contours of the mediational picture become clearly visible, and the principle unifying otherwise very different mediational views stands out.

But for those still embedded in the mediational view, all this is far from evident. They often see themselves as having rejected and refuted the early Cartesian or empiricist epistemologies, and are surprised and not a little pained to hear that they are portrayed as the heirs of Descartes. Hence a debate breaks out as to who has really confuted classical epistemology. From one side, figures like Richard Rorty and Donald Davidson claim to have done so, but are seen by those who stand within the post-Hegelian line of deconstruction as being still enmired in mediationalism. On another side, these deconstructors can seem to be still in the same traditional grooves, because they are still raising questions about the conditions of experience, instead of dropping them altogether as futile and misleading.[16]

Rorty, for instance, has a distinctive stance in the contemporary philosophical world. It is one that is often described as "antirealist," "relativist," "subjectivist." But Rorty repudiates such labels. His point rather is that we should get away from a number of philosophical dichotomies which have supposedly outlived their usefulness; we should learn that we can lay them to rest, that they add nothing of value to our thought. Somewhat overmodestly describing himself with the Lockean term "underlaborer," he sees himself as "clean[ing] up and dispos[ing] of what [great] imaginative pioneers [e.g., Frege and Mill, Russell and Heidegger, Dewey and Habermas, Davidson and Derrida] have shown to be rubbish."[17]

---

16. Charles Taylor has treated this debate and its cross-purposes in "Overcoming Epistemology," chap. 1 in *Philosophical Arguments* (Cambridge, MA: Harvard University Press, 1995).

17. Richard Rorty, *Truth and Progress*, vol. 3 of *Philosophical Papers* (Cambridge: Cambridge University Press, 1998), 8.

Now we, as followers of Heidegger and Merleau-Ponty, find this hard to accept. Rorty and Charles Taylor in fact debated this back and forth for some time. What has been constant throughout the debate is that both sides see themselves as getting out from under the Cartesian representational epistemology, and see the other side as imprisoned in it. For Rorty we escape from "the collapsed circus tent of epistemology—those acres of canvas under which many of our colleagues still thrash aimlessly about"[18]—mainly by getting rid of certain traditional distinctions and questions, like, for instance, the scheme/content way of talking, or the issue of correspondence with reality; while we think that these questions and distinctions have to be recast. Rorty is a minimalist: he thinks we had best just forget about the whole range of issues that concern how our thought relates to reality, the relation of Mind and World, if we can relapse again into those great uppercase terms about which Rorty likes to wax ironic. We are maximalists: we think that our colleagues must retain the issues but badly need to recast their distorted understanding of these matters, inherited from the epistemological tradition.

Our reason is that you can't just walk away from these deep, pervasive, half-articulated, taken-for-granted pictures which are embedded in our culture and enframe our thought and action. You can't free yourself from them until you identify them, and see where they're wrong, and even then it's not always easy. Just saying you've abandoned them, and then not giving them any thought, à la Davidson and Rorty, is a sure recipe for remaining in their thrall.

How to pursue this debate further? How to show that the mediational picture is alive if unwell? One way would be to start with the agreed basis, underlying our difference, and see how best to understand it. Now what we certainly agree on is that the foundationalist enterprise that Descartes launched is misguided. Indeed, antifoundationalism seems the received wisdom of our time. Almost everyone seems to agree that the great enterprise of Descartes, to build up certain knowledge from undeniable building blocks, is misconceived. Everyone from Quine to Heidegger, passing through various postmodernists, can sign on to this conclusion.

And yet this wide agreement hides yawning disparities in outlook. There is in fact more than one antifoundationalist argument; and the different

18. Ibid.

approaches start from quite different basic ideas, and generate very different conclusions, and quite divergent anthropological and political consequences. Moreover, the different ways of conceiving the common antifoundationalist thesis account for most of the major differences in outlook. Understanding antifoundationalism as they do, each looks at the others as betraying a grievous lack of understanding of the common point.

But what is the point? On our view, Cartesian-Lockean foundationalism breaks down because the certainty-producing argument would have to proceed from establishing elements (whatever else is true, I'm *sure* that: red, here, now) to grounding wholes; but you can't isolate elements in the way you would have to for this to work. A certain holism gets in the way. But buyer beware! Holisms come in practically as many flavors as Baskin-Robbins ice cream, and this one is *not* the Quine-Davidson holism. That is a holism of verification first of all; it reflects that propositions or claims in a certain domain can't be verified singly. It is only derivatively a holism about meaning, insofar as attributions of meaning in the observed agent's speech amount to claims, which, like most others, can't be verified singly, but only in packages with other claims.

In other words, Quinean holism is a thesis which applies even after accepting the classical Cartesian empiricist doctrine of the atomism of the input. But Davidson's theory is basically similar. When I learn someone else's language—develop a "theory of meaning" to interpret his utterances—I can only do so holistically. To learn that this particular sound ("gavagai") is his word for "rabbit," I have to accept as true a number of other claims about the meanings of his utterances, as well as his desires and beliefs, and all these together have to make sense of his actions and speech. Suppose he is shouting excitedly "blook gavagai," and pointing in the direction of this rabbit hopping towards the woods. Together with the supposition that "blook" means "get," as well as the supposition that he's hungry, likes eating rabbits, needs my help to catch this one for lunch, etc., we have very strong reason to believe that this new word, "gavagai," that we haven't heard before, means "rabbit."

But suppose that this people never eat rabbits, that our interlocutor isn't hungry, that he is a priest, that the wood the rabbit is running towards is a sacred grove, and all small furry mammals are lumped together by this tribe in a category of the "unclean." The excitement is not about anticipating a delicious meal, but about the possible desecration consequent on this animal setting foot in the grove. Then "gavagai" doesn't translate our "rabbit," but perhaps "unclean beast," or "small furry mammal."

Here we have a Quine-type holism, applied to this particular case of radical interpretation. You can never verify a single meaning equivalence on its own, but only in the context of a whole set of other suppositions about the target language, and the beliefs and desires of its speakers. Similarly, when something goes wrong with the communication, when we think we respond to a request, and produce anger instead of satisfaction, there is always more than one of our hitherto accepted suppositions which may have to be changed in order to understand our interlocutor properly. Acting under the first supposition, that he is hungry, I chase the rabbit and dive at it, grabbing it, but also sliding with it into the woods. To my chagrin, this helpful act is met with horror and consternation. Puzzled, I wonder whether my interlocutor didn't want me to grab something else. It may take me a long time to figure out what's going on here.

But now note that this (very valid and important) holistic thesis supposes an atomism of the input; that is, it tells me how I have to relate a number of facts and suppositions, which can be identified (although not verified) independently of each other. The man is excitedly uttering *"blook gavagai,"* there is a rabbit running across the clearing, he is pointing in its direction; these combine with other suppositions which I have gleaned earlier: these people eat rabbits, it's been a long time since breakfast, etc. Given all these elements, Davidson tells us how they have to be combined in order to yield a valid theory of meaning for this speaker (viz., according to the principle of charity: make his sentences generally true, and his deliberations rational). But the elements themselves are givens. That is what we mean in speaking of a holism of verification.

Now the holism we're invoking here is more radical. We might call it a "gestalt holism." The point has often been made about gestalts that they can't be seen as simply composed of their parts. Or to put the point in another way, the meaningful elements they contain cannot be identified on their own, but only in relation to the whole. This high note is the climax of a long rising passage in this song. But its nature as climax doesn't reside in the note itself. The same note in another song has a quite different valence. This kind of holism undercuts completely the atomism of the input. These elements are what they are only in relation to the whole and to each other. It is not that, independently identified, they have to be combined in a certain way in order to yield truth. It is independent identification as such which is impossible.

We can note that in talking about gestalt holism, we fell into using such terms as "meaning" and "valence." Gestalts are meaningful wholes. And this brings us back to the holisms which stand in the lineage descending from Kant's move that we described above. These holisms purport to refute atomism, first because the nature of any given element is determined by its "meaning" (*Sinn, sens*), which can only be defined by placing it in a larger whole, and second, and even worse, because the larger whole itself isn't just an aggregation of such elements.[19]

To make this second point slightly clearer: the "elements" which could figure in a foundationalist reconstruction of knowledge are bits of explicit information (red, here, now; or "there's a rabbit" ["gavagai"]). But the whole which allows these to have the sense they have is a "world," a locus of shared understanding organized by social practice. I notice the rabbit, because I pick it out against the stable background of those trees and this open space before them. Without having found my feet in the place, there could be no rabbit sighting. If the whole stage on which the rabbit darts out were uncertain, say swirling around as it is when I am about to faint, there could be no registering of this explicit bit of information. But my having found my feet in this locus is not a matter of my having extra bits of explicit information— that is, it can never just consist in this, although other bits may be playing a role. It is an exercise of my ability to cope, something I have acquired as this bodily being brought up in this culture.

So "holism" in some form is a generally agreed thesis among antifoundationalists. All the trouble arises when each one of us spells out what seems obviously to follow from this; or makes clearer what seems evidently to be

19. Part of the confusion surrounding Davidson's work comes from the fact that he is proposing a "theory of meaning," which might seem to align his views with Gestalt holism. But "meaning" itself has different senses in the two contexts. Davidson is proposing a theory of linguistic meaning, which is moreover "designative" in our sense; that is, it defines the meanings of linguistic expressions through the way the sentences in which they figure relate to features of the world as their truth conditions. But the meaningful elements of a gestalt possess *Sinn* or *sens* not in virtue of their relations to what stands outside them, but in relation to each other, and the whole they form together. It is, of course, no accident that Merleau-Ponty makes prominent use of Gestalt theory in his account of our *être-au-monde*.

the nature of this holistic background. What seems evident to one seems wildly implausible to others.

Our spelling out involves something like this. Our ability to cope can be seen as incorporating an overall sense of ourselves and our world; which sense includes and is carried by a spectrum of rather different abilities: at one end, beliefs which we hold, which may or may not be "in our minds" at the moment; at the other, abilities to get around and deal intelligently with things. Intellectualism has made us see these as very different sites; but philosophy in our day has shown how closely akin they are, and how interlinked.

Heidegger has taught us to speak of our ability to get around as a kind of "understanding" of our world. And indeed, drawing a sharp line between this implicit grasp on things and our formulated, explicit understanding is impossible. It is not only that any frontier is porous, that things explicitly formulated and understood can with practice become assimilated to unarticulated know-how, in the way that Hubert and Stuart Dreyfus have shown us with learning;[20] and that our grasp on things can move as well in the other direction, as we articulate what was previously just lived out. It is also that any particular understanding of our situation blends explicit knowledge and unarticulated know-how.

I am informed that a tiger has escaped from the local zoo, and now as I walk through the wood behind my house, the recesses of the forest stand out for me differently, they take on a new valence, my environment now is traversed by new lines of force, in which the vectors of possible attack have an important place. My sense of this environment takes on a new shape, thanks to this new bit of information.

So the whole in which particular things are understood, and bits of information taken in, is a sense of my world, carried in a plurality of media: formulated thoughts, but also things never even raised as a question, but taken as a framework in which the formulated thoughts have the sense they do (e.g., the never-questioned overall shape of things, which keeps me from even entertaining the kind of weird conjectures discussed in Chapter 1, such as that the world started five minutes ago, or that it suddenly stops beyond

20. Hubert Dreyfus and Stuart Dreyfus, *Mind over Machine* (New York: Free Press, 1986, paperback 2nd revised edition, 1988).

my door), as well as the understanding implicit in various abilities to cope. As in the multimedia world of our culture, although some parts of our grasp of things clearly fit one medium rather than others (my knowing Weber's theory of capitalism, my being able to ride a bicycle), in fact the boundaries between media are very fuzzy, and many of the most important understandings are multimedia events, as when I stroll through the potentially tiger-infested wood. Moreover, in virtue of the holism which reigns here, every bit of my understanding draws on the whole, and is in this indirect way a multimedia understanding.

Maybe we're still saying things with which all antifoundationalists agree. But very soon, we come to further inferences where we part ways. For instance, it seems to us that this picture of the background rules out what we've been calling a representational or mediational picture of our grasp of the world. For it is a feature of this mediational view, with its distinction of outer and inner, that we can understand our grasp of the world as something which is in principle separable from what it is a grasp of.

This separation was obviously central to the original Cartesian thrust which we are all trying to turn back and deconstruct. On one side, there were the bits of putative information in the mind—ideas, impressions, sense-data; on the other, there was the "outside world" about which these claimed to inform us. The dualism can later take other, more sophisticated forms, as we saw. Representations can be reconceived, no longer as "ideas," but as sentences, in keeping with the linguistic turn, as we see with Quine. Or the dualism itself can be fundamentally reconceptualized, as with Kant. Instead of being defined in terms of original and copy, it is seen on the model of form and content, mold and filling.

In whatever form, mediational theories posit something which can be defined as inner, as our contribution to knowing, and which can be distinguished from what is out there. Hence these theories can also be called "inside/outside" accounts (I/O for short).

And hence also the continuance of skeptical questions, or their permutations: Maybe the world doesn't really conform to the representation? Or: maybe we will come across others whose molds are irreducibly different from ours, with whom we shall therefore be unable to establish any common standards of truth? This underlies much facile relativism in our day.

But a reflection on our whole multimedia grasp of things ought to put paid to this dualism once and for all. If we stare at the medium of explicit belief, then the separation can seem plausible. My beliefs about the moon can be held, even actualized in my present thinking, even if the moon isn't now visible—perhaps even though it doesn't exist, if it turns out to be a fiction. But the grasp of things involved in my ability to move around and manipulate objects can't be divided up like that. Because unlike moon-beliefs, this ability can't be actualized in the absence of the objects it operates on. My ability to throw baseballs can't be exercised in the absence of baseballs. My ability to get around this city, this house comes out only in getting around this city and house.

We might be tempted to say: it doesn't exist in my mind like my theoretical beliefs, but in the ability to move which I have in my whole body. But that understates the embedding. The locus here is the ability to move-in-this-environment. It exists not just in my body, but in my body-walking-the-streets. Similarly, my ability to be charming or seductive exists not in my body and voice, but in body-and-voice-in-conversation-with-an-interlocutor.

Merleau-Ponty takes a skilled football player as his paradigm case of how an embodied agent is geared into the situation. "For the player in action the football field is . . . pervaded with lines of force (the 'yard lines'; those which demarcate the 'penalty area') and articulated in sectors (for example, the 'openings' between the adversaries) which call for a certain mode of action and which initiate and guide the action as if the player were unaware of it. The field itself is not given to him, but present as the immanent term of his practical intentions; the player becomes one with it and feels the direction of the 'goal,' for example, just as immediately as the vertical and the horizontal planes of his own body."[21]

Merleau-Ponty then provides a general account of the way we are in direct touch with the things with which we are dealing. In all such cases our coping is experienced as a steady flow of skillful activity in response to our sense of the situation. Part of that experience is a sense of whether or not coping is going well. When one senses a deviation from some optimal body-environment gestalt, one's activity takes one closer to an optimal body-environment relationship that relieves the "tension." But that final gestalt

21. Maurice Merlau-Ponty, *The Structure of Behavior*, trans. Alden L. Fisher, (Boston: Beacon, 1967), 168–169.

need not be represented in the agent's brain or mind. He is simply drawn to respond in a way that is likely to lower his sense of tension or disequilibrium. As Merleau-Ponty puts it, "Our body is not an object for an 'I think', it is a grouping of lived-through meanings which moves towards its equilibrium."[22] Thus, skillful coping does not require any representation of a *goal*. It can be *purposive* without the agent entertaining a *purpose*. According to Merleau-Ponty: "To move one's body is to aim at things through it; it is to allow oneself to respond to their call, which is made upon it independently of any representation."[23]

To distinguish this unmediated body-based intentionality from representational intentionality, Merleau-Ponty calls the body's response to the ongoing situation *motor intentionality*.[24] To see that and how motor intentionality is more basic than representational intentionality and makes it possible, it is instructive to contrast Merleau-Ponty and John Searle on action.

Searle claims that for a bodily movement to be an action it must be caused by an intention in action—a propositional representation of the action's conditions of satisfaction. Searle assumes that, in all cases of comportment, the agent must be able to recognize in advance what would count as success and that this representation of the goal is separable from the action. That is, I may fail to achieve my goal in the world, but this does not affect my having *in mind* the intention to achieve it. Here we encounter the I/O distinction again, this time in the domain of action.

If we return to the phenomenon of absorbed coping, however, we can see that, although Searle has correctly described the intentionality of trying to achieve a goal, absorbed coping does not require that the agent's movements be governed by a representation of its success conditions. Rather, as we have just seen, the agent's absorbed response to the solicitations of the situation must lower a tension without his knowing in advance how to reach equilibrium and what it would feel like to do so. Thus, besides Searle's success conditions, the

22. Ibid., 153.

23. Ibid., 139. To help convince us that no representation of the final gestalt is needed for the skilled performer to move towards it, Merleau-Ponty uses the analogy of a soap bubble. The bubble starts as a deformed film. The bits of soap respond to local forces according to laws that happen to work so as to dispose the entire system to end up as a sphere, but the spherical result does not play a causal role in producing the bubble.

24. Ibid., 110.

phenomenologist is led to introduce what one might call conditions of improvement. What Searle's I/O picture does not allow him to see is that motor intentionality is directly sensitive to *conditions of improvement* in the world and so does not need to represent the activity's *conditions of satisfaction.*

To deal with the way everyday skills seem to involve movements that are not caused by intentions in action, Searle introduces what he calls the background of capacities, abilities, and so forth. Although Searle's recognition of the necessity of explaining skillful coping by supplementing the representational intention in action distinguishes him from the pure representationalist, it does not ultimately free him from the I/O picture. He insists that absorbed coping is not itself a kind of intentionality but rather that "intentionality rises to the level of background abilities."[25] This slogan suggests that, in acting, the agent has to have in mind (or at least be able to have in mind) what he is trying to do, and that everything else required to carry out the action must be understood as nonrepresentational background capacities that cause subsidiary movements that do not themselves have conditions of satisfaction. This move is typical of the representationalist. When the phenomenon in question can't be accounted for by mental representations, in this case the intention in action, the only alternative seems to be that whatever else is going on in skillful action cannot be meaningful, and must, therefore, be the effect of meaningless, mechanical causes.

But this analysis leaves us with a new problem. Since each movement involved in an action does not have its own conditions of satisfaction, it should not have intentionality, yet, as Searle points out, each subsidiary movement is done intentionally. Searle's solution is that, to be intentional, each subsidiary movement of an action must be somehow caused by the relevant intention in action. As Searle puts it: "Intentionality reaches down to the bottom level of voluntary actions. Thus, for example, the skillful skier has his Intentionality at the level of getting down the mountain. But each subsidiary movement is nonetheless an intentional movement. Each movement is governed by the Intentionality of the flow."[26]

But this "reaching down and governing" remains completely mysterious.

25. John R. Searle, "Response: The Background of Intentionality and Action," in *John Searle and His Critics*, ed. E. Lepore and R. Van Gulick (Cambridge: Basil Blackwell, 1991), 293.
26. Ibid.

Once we pay attention to the phenomenon of skilled activity, however, it becomes clear that the intention in action need not reach down and directly govern the flow. Rather than a representation of the action's success conditions directly governing the agent's subsidiary movements, a sense of the conditions of improvement could take over the job as the agent felt drawn to lower the current tension. The intention in action would then be merely an occasion that triggered the more basic motor intentionality in which the body is motivated to respond directly to the situation.

Thus, ongoing coping supplies the basis for all goal-directed activity. Moreover, motor intentionality cannot be explained in terms of physical causation because it involves a sense of being solicited to do what feels appropriate, nor can it be understood as the result of mental causality as when an intention in action causes a bodily movement, precisely because it is presupposed in order to account for the way a mental representation, in this case an intention in action, can indirectly move the body. In short, motor intentionality makes representational intentionality possible.

Living with things involves a certain kind of understanding (which we might also call "preunderstanding"). That is, things figure for us in their meaning or relevance for our purposes, desires, activities. As I navigate my way along the path up the hill, my mind totally absorbed anticipating the difficult conversation I'm going to have at my destination, I treat the different features of the terrain as obstacles, supports, openings, invitations to tread more warily or run freely, etc. Even when I'm not thinking of them these things have those relevances for me; I know my way about among them.

This is nonconceptual; put another way, language isn't playing any direct role. Through language, we (humans) have the capacity to focus on things, to pick an X out *as* X; we pick it out as something which (correctly) bears a description "X," and this puts our identification in the domain of potential critique (Is this really an X? Is the vocabulary to which X belongs the appropriate one for this domain/purpose? etc.). At some point, because of some breakdown, or just through intrinsic interest, I may come to focus on some aspects of this navigational know-how. I may begin to classify things as "obstacles" or "facilitations," and this will change the way I live in the world. But in all sorts of ways, I live in the world and deal with it, without having done this.

Ordinary coping isn't conceptual. But at the same time, it can't be understood in just inanimate-causal terms. This denial can be understood in two ways. Maximally, it runs athwart a common ambition of, for example, cognitivism, which aims precisely to give one day a reductive account of experience in terms of formal symbolic representations. In the 1980s a model-free nonrepresentational machine-learning algorithm, called actor-critic temporal difference reinforcement learning, was proposed and was shown to learn to play backgammon at expert level. Based on such successes, neural accounts have recently been developed that explain coping in neural terms and show how the brain can guide behavior without recourse to representations.[27] This would show that phenomenologists and neuroscientists are converging on a nonmentalistic account of situational skillful coping. This model-free account of the brain basis of skillful coping converges with, and supports, our contact phenomenology of skillful action.

In any case, in the absence of this promised but far-distant mechanistic account, our only way of making sense of animals, and of our own preconceptual goings-on, is through something like preunderstanding. That is, we have to see the world impinging on these beings in relevance terms; or alternatively put, we see them and ourselves as active.

We find it impossible not to extend this courtesy to animals, as we have just indicated. But in our case, the reasons are stronger. When we focus on some feature of our dealing with the world and bring it to speech, it doesn't

---

27. Neuroscience has established that procedural coping ability is produced by a system of brain areas centered on the subcortical basal ganglia, including cortico-striatal loops with, in addition, connections with limbic areas such as the amygdala. The limbic system provides *reward* signals needed for the experiential reinforcement learning of skill. Reward expressed by the limbic system's secretion of neural modulars, such as dopamine, is the body's emotional response to how an encounter with the world is evolving or has terminated. This reward system requires that the brain be embodied and cannot be divorced from its involvement with the world. The prefrontal cortical part of this system seems to be involved in providing appropriate saliencing. This saliencing creates a foreground-background distinction that is necessary for an organism to act in accordance with what is variously called, depending upon the context and researcher, a goal, a task, a set, a sense of the situation, a disposition to action, a *perspective*. See Stuart Dreyfus, "System 0: The Overlooked Explanation of Expert Intuition," in *Handbook of Research Methods on Intuition*, ed. M. Sinclair (Cheltenham: Edward Elgar Publishers, 2014), 15–27.

come across as just like a discovery of some unsuspected fact, like, for example, the change in landscape at a turn in the road, or being informed that what we do bears some fancy technical name (M. Jourdain speaking prose[28]). When I finally allow myself to recognize that what has been making me uncomfortable in this conversation is that I'm feeling jealous, I feel that in a sense I wasn't totally ignorant of this before. I knew it without knowing it. It has a kind of intermediate status between known and quite unknown. It was a kind of protoknowledge, an environment propitious for the transformation that conceptual focus brings, even though there may also have been resistances.

We have been drawing in the above on Heidegger, as well as on the work of Merleau-Ponty. We find in both of them this idea that our conceptual thinking is "embedded" in everyday coping. The point of this image can be taken in two bites, as it were. The first is that coping is prior and pervasive (*zunächst und zumeist*). We start off just as coping infants, and only later are inducted into speech. And even as adults, much of our lives consists in this coping. This couldn't be otherwise. In order to focus on something, we have to keep going—as I was on the path, while thinking of the difficult conversation; or as the person is in the laboratory, walking around, picking up the retort, while thinking hard about the theoretical issues (or maybe, what's for lunch).

But the second bite goes deeper. It's the point usually expressed with the term "background." The mass of coping is an essential support to the episodes of conceptual focus in our lives, not just in the infrastructural sense that something has to be carrying our mind around from library to laboratory and back. More fundamentally, the background understanding we need to make the sense we do of the pieces of thinking we engage in resides in our ordinary coping.

I walk up the path and enter the field and notice: the goldenrod is out. A particulate take on the world, which are often understood as elementary boundary according to the I/O; except that under the pressure of foundationalism, they sometimes are forced to be more basic—yellow here now— and only build up to goldenrod as a later inference. One of the errors of classical epistemology was to see in this kind of take the building blocks of

28. Moliere, *Le Bourgeois Gentilhomme* (Paris: Pierre Bordas, 1977).

our knowledge of the world. We put it together bit by bit out of such pieces. So foundationalism had to believe.

One of the reasons that Kant is a crucial figure in the (oh-so-laborious) overcoming of the I/O—even though he also created his own version of it—is that he put paid to this picture, as we argued above. We can't build our view of the world out of percepts like "the goldenrod is out," or even "yellow here now," because nothing would count as such a percept unless it already had its place in a world. Minimally, nothing could be a *percept* without a surrounding sense of myself as perceiving agent, moving in some surroundings, of which this bit of yellow is a feature. If we try to think all this orientation away, then we get something which is close to unthinkable as an experience, "less even than a dream," as Kant puts it.[29] What would it be like just to experience yellow, never mind whether it's somewhere in the world out there or just in my head? A very dissociated experience, and not a very promising building block for a worldview.

So our understanding of the world is holistic from the start, in a sense different from the Quinean one. There is no such thing as the single, independent percept. Something has this status only within a wider context which is understood, taken for granted, but for the most part not focused on. Moreover, it couldn't all be focused on, not just because it is very widely ramifying, but because it doesn't consist of some definite number of pieces. We can bring this out by reflecting that the number of ways in which the taken-for-granted background could in specific circumstances fail is not delimitable.

Invoking this undelimitable background was a favorite argumentative gambit of Wittgenstein in both the *Investigations* and *On Certainty*. As we indicated above, he shows, for instance, that understanding an ostensive definition is not just a matter of fixing a particular; there is a whole surrounding understanding of what kind of thing is being discussed (the shape or the color), of this being a way of teaching meaning, and the like. In our ordinary investigations, we take for granted a continuing world—so that our whole proceedings would be radically undercut by the "discovery," if one could make it, that the universe started five minutes ago. But that can't be taken to mean that there is a definite list of things that we have ruled out, including among others that the universe started five minutes ago.

29. Kant, *Kritik*, A112.

Now this indefinitely extending background understanding is sustained and evolved through our ordinary coping. My recognition that the goldenrod is out is sustained by a context being in place, for example that I'm now entering a field, and it's August. And I'm not focusing on all this. I know where I am, because I walked here, and when I am because I've been living through the summer, but these are not reflective inferences; they are just part of the understanding I have in everyday coping. I might indeed take a more reflective stance, and theorize the existence of goldenrod in certain geographical locations of the earth's surface in a certain season, etc., just as I might lay out the environment I normally walk about in by drawing a map. But this wouldn't end the embedding of reflective knowledge in ordinary coping. The map becomes useless, indeed ceases to be a map in any meaningful sense for me, unless I can use it to help me get around. Theoretical knowledge has to be situated in relation to everyday coping to be the knowledge that it is.

In this way, embedding is inescapable, and that in the stronger sense: that all exercises of reflective, conceptual thought only have the content they have situated in a context of background understanding which underlies and is generated in everyday coping.

CHAPTER THREE

Checking Beliefs

NOW THE DIFFERENCE between an antifoundationalism that breaks with the mediational view of knowledge, and one which does not, may seem relatively minor. After all, they both agree in abandoning the original Cartesian enterprise. But in fact, a great deal of the Cartesian philosophical outlook survives if you don't break with the representational epistemology.

We can see this if we look at the whole complex of issues around "realism" and "antirealism." The mediational view provides the context in which these questions make sense. They lose this sense if you escape from this construal, as Heidegger and Merleau-Ponty have done. Or perhaps better put, one awakes to an unproblematic realism, no longer a daring philosophical "thesis."

It has often been noticed how mediationalism leads, by recoil, to skepticism, relativism, and various forms of nonrealism. Once the foundationalist arguments for establishing truth are seen to fail, we are left with the image of the self-enclosed subject, out of contact with the transcendent world. And this easily generates theses of the unknowable (e.g., *Dingen an sich*), of the privacy of thought (the private language argument), or of relativism. More particularly in this last case, the picture of each mind acceding to the world from behind the screen of its own percepts, or grasping it in molds of its own making, seems to offer no way of rational arbitration of disputes. How can the protagonists base their arguments on commonly available elements, when each is encased within his or her own picture?

Starting from skepticism[1] or relativism, the move is obvious and tempting to adopt some mode of antirealism. If these questions can't be rationally arbitrated, then why accept that they are real questions? Why agree that there is a fact of the matter here to be right or wrong about? If we can never know whether our language, or ideas, or categories correspond to the reality out there, the things-in-themselves, then what warrant have we to talk about this transcendent reality in the first place? We have to deny it the status of the "real." Hence "antirealism."

The crucial move of these nonrealisms is to deny some basic common-sense distinctions between reality and our picture of it: the world as it is versus the world as we see it, what is really morally right versus what we think right, and so on. The irony is that this denies distinctions which were first erected into dichotomies by the representational construal.

Now it is obvious that foundationalism is in a sense in the same dialectical universe as nonrealism, that set up by mediational theories. These theories raise the fear that our representations might be just in the mind, out of touch with reality (even that we might be the victims of an evil genius [*malin genie*]). Foundationalism is an answer to such fears. That is why there is often such an indignant reaction in our scientific-philosophical community to various relativist or nonrealist theories—and, incidentally, to Rorty as the supposed propounder of such. This is because the whole culture is in the grip of a mediationalist perspective, and therefore can entertain the nightmare of being irremediably out of touch with the real. But science seems to depend on our not being so out of touch; so whoever flirts with such theories is against science, giving aid and comfort to the enemy, destroying our civilization, and so on, and so on.

Rorty rightly doesn't allow himself to be fazed by such Blimpish reactions. But his way of dealing with them shows that he is still in the same

---

1. We are talking here about general skepticism. There is also a more specific form which targets science, while sparing ordinary everyday reality. We will deal with this targeted form below, in Chapter 7.

mental universe in crucial ways. The kind of mediationalism that is relevant here takes as mediating elements what one could call "representations." "Representations" in the meaning of the act are formulated or explicit bits of knowledge, as these have figured in foundationalist-epistemological theories. How mediation has been conceived has varied, as we explained in Chapter 1. For Descartes and Locke the crucial elements were "ideas," particulate mental contents, hovering on the boundary between little copy-objects in the mind, and knowledge claims which could only be captured in that-clauses. Later Kant claimed that the minimal form of such content involved some subsumptive judgement. Some theorists tried to get these basic units out of the mind and into the material body—hence the "surface irritations"[2] of Quine. But in the twentieth century, with the linguistic turn, the basic unit has come to be something like sentences held true, or beliefs.

Now we're calling "representationalists" those who think that our knowledge consists exclusively of representations, and that our reasoning involves manipulating representations. To speak the language of Sellars and McDowell, they hold that the only inhabitants of the space of reasons are beliefs. In other words, they are people who have (in our view) failed to take on board the Heidegger or Merleau-Ponty point about the embedding of our explicit beliefs in our background grasp of things.

(Of course, one can *define* the space of reasons as consisting only of beliefs; and this even makes a certain sense, when we think of reason*ing*, the giving of grounds for our beliefs. But this narrow definition leaves out the way in which we *form* beliefs in perception, which we will be discussing immediately below. It would be a catastrophic mistake to include this in the space of *causes*, whereas it provides essential support for all our reasoning about the world.)

Now in this sense, Rorty, following Davidson, is still representationalist. Thus Davidson says: "What distinguishes a coherence theory is simply the claim that nothing can count as a reason for holding a belief except another belief."[3] And he makes it clear that in this sense he wants to endorse a coherence theory, albeit claiming that it is compatible with what is true

2. W. V. O. Quine, "Scope and Language of Science," in *The Ways of Paradox, and Other Essays* (Cambridge, MA: Harvard University Press, 1976).

3. Donald Davidson, "A Coherence Theory of Truth and Knowledge," in *Truth and Interpretation: Perspectives on the Philosophy of Donald Davidson*, ed. Ernest LePore (Oxford: Blackwell, 1992), 310.

in a correspondence theory. In the same passage, Davidson quotes Rorty approvingly: "Nothing counts as justification unless by reference to what we already accept, and there is no way to get outside our beliefs and language so as to find some test other than coherence."[4] The two seem to be in agreement on this.[5] Indeed, this stance and the connected sharp distinction between causation and justification seem to be an essential part of Rorty's strategy in this domain.

This is clearly a representationalist view. Beliefs are the only accepted denizens of the space of reasons. But we want to note something more here. This view is not put forward as a surprising finding. It is articulated as a truism. *Of course* nothing can justify a belief except another one. Why is this so obvious? Because, dummy, the only way you could find an alternative would be to "get outside our beliefs and language." Davidson makes the same point in talking of the possible alternative of confronting our beliefs "with the tribunal of experience. No such confrontation makes sense, for of course we can't get outside our skins to find out what is causing the internal happenings of which we are aware."[6]

What we want to bring out here is the way that both philosophers lean on the basic lineaments of the mediational picture in order to show their thesis to be obvious. "We can't get outside." This is the basic image of the I/O. We are contained within our own representations, and can't stand somehow beyond them to compare them with "reality." This is the standard picture, out of which nonrealist theories were generated in the first place. And here we find it invoked within an argument which is meant to repudiate that picture. This is what it means to be held captive.

To show how this coherentist claim is so far from obvious as to be plain false, we need to step outside the mediational picture, and think in terms of the kind of embedded knowing which Heidegger and Merleau-Ponty have thematized. Of course we check our claims against reality. "Johnny, go into the room and tell me whether the picture is crooked." Johnny does as he is told. He doesn't check the (problematized) belief that the picture is crooked against his own belief. He emerges from the room with a view of the matter,

    4. Rorty, *Philosophy and the Mirror of Nature*, 178.
    5. See also Robert Brandom's account of Rorty's position in the introduction to *Rorty and His Critics*, ed. Robert Brandom (Oxford: Blackwell, 2000), xiv.
    6. Davidson, "A Coherence Theory," 312.

but checking isn't comparing the problematized belief with his view of the matter; checking is forming a belief about the matter, in this case by going and looking.

This sounds like a simple enough task, but, in fact, it presupposes the mastery of a daunting ensemble of skills we share with all higher organisms. To look at something, we need to make the indeterminate scene before us determinate, stabilize the background, focus on an object, and optimize the viewing conditions. Seeing only seems a simple operation because we have gotten so good at it that, as long as things are going normally, we no longer notice what we are doing. But we can look at various breakdown cases to catch ourselves in the process of perceiving. Merleau-Ponty's original and important contribution in *Phenomenology of Perception* is to use such cases to call our attention to the complex interaction of the perceptual field, things, and what he calls the body schema in the constitution of the objects of perception.

To begin with we need to make the scene before us determinate. Normally, this stage has become so natural for us that it takes place almost instantaneously, but we can notice it in unusual cases. Merleau-Ponty gives the example of seeing what first appears to be an indeterminate and unstable scene: "If I walk along a shore towards a ship which has run aground, and the funnel or masts merge into the forest bordering on the sand dune, there will be a moment when these details suddenly become part of the ship, and indissolubly fused with it. As I approached, I did not perceive resemblances or proximities which finally came together to form a continuous picture of the upper part of the ship. I merely felt that the look of the object was on the point of altering, that something was imminent in this tension, as a storm is imminent in storm clouds. Suddenly the sight before me was recast in a manner satisfying to my vague expectation."[7]

As the scene before us sorts itself into determinate objects, it also organizes into a figure on a background. Then, our body schema operates automatically, as if we had a skill we had always already learned, to stabilize the background. In the case of vision, that includes setting the level of illumination and keeping our experience of its brightness constant over a wide range of objective

---

7. Maurice Merleau-Ponty, *Phenomenology of Perception*, trans. Donald Landes (London: Routledge, 2013), 17.

changes of intensity. Thus, if we are engaged in some activity, even though the light, as measured on a light meter, gets dimmer and dimmer, the perceived illumination stays constant, until, to our surprise, we are working in almost total darkness. Likewise, the color of objects continues to look constant through a wide range of objective changes in the color of the illumination, as we notice when pictures we took near sunset of what seemed naturally colored scenes come back from the developer looking orange, or when an electrically lit interior that looked yellowish from outside on a snowy day, looks neutral as soon as our body enters the incandescent light. Our sense of the vertical dimension of a scene is established and preserved in the same way. Merleau-Ponty draws on Gestaltist experiments to report that, if a subject who is wearing goggles to invert his perception of the world is allowed to move around and deal with things, after an initial period of disorientation the world rights itself so that he can even ski and ride a bicycle.

So much for the background constancies or levels as Merleau-Ponty calls them. Meanwhile, the figure too is being stabilized. Objects are given as having a constant size as we approach them, even though their image on the retina is rapidly expanding. Merleau-Ponty points out that, since a camera, unlike an embodied and mobile subject, does not maintain size constancy, in a movie a train looks like it is rapidly growing large as it approaches; for the same reason, noses or feet near the camera are grossly enlarged. Size constancy breaks down only when we no longer have a sense of how we could move to grasp the object. Thus we see what look like toy cars and houses from a plane. Likewise, the body schema keeps the shape and color of objects constant even though the actual color of an object is affected by the color of nearby objects, and the shape of the object as projected on the retina changes as we move around it. To help us see this remarkable work of perceptual organization we normally accomplish without noticing it, Merleau-Ponty describes how Cézanne, by painting a still life in many colors and from many perspectives, attempted to give viewers a sense of objects coming into stable color and shape, and thus give them a sense of the reality of the object more convincing than that of Renaissance perspective or impressionist attempts to paint the light itself.

> The contour of an object conceived as a line encircling the object belongs not to the visible world but to geometry. If one outlines the shape of an apple with

a continuous line, one makes an object of the shape, whereas the contour is rather the ideal limit toward which the sides of the apple recede in depth. Not to indicate any shape would be to deprive the objects of their identity. To trace just a single outline sacrifices depth—that is, the dimension in which the thing is presented not as spread out before us but as an inexhaustible reality full of reserves. That is why Cézanne follows the swell of the object in modulated colors and indicates *several* outlines in blue. Rebounding among these, one's glance captures a shape that emerges from among them all, just as it does in perception.[8]

Finally, we each learn the skill of positioning ourselves so as to obtain an optimal grip on the perceptual scene. We have already seen how, in action, we develop a skill of moving so that our anticipations are continually realized. Merleau-Ponty points out a special way such movement functions in perception. Normally, when we first see an object we sense our distance from it as a disequilibrium that we can correct by moving so as to get a better look. We are thus led to seek a vantage point from which we can take in the thing as a whole as well as its details. As Merleau-Ponty puts it, summing up the role of the tendency towards gaining a maximal grip in both action and perception: "My body is geared into the world when my perception presents me with a spectacle as varied and as clearly articulated as possible, and when my motor intentions, as they unfold, receive the responses they expect from the world. This maximum sharpness of perception and action points clearly to a perceptual *ground*, a basis of my life, a general setting in which my body can co-exist with the world."[9]

Of course, in perception, as in action, since we are experts in viewing objects, our movement to the optimal viewing point usually happens almost instantly and outside our attention. And, again, Merleau-Ponty brilliantly finds a case where such skilled activity is slowed down so that it can be noticed. He reminds us: "For each object, as for each picture in an art gallery, there is an optimal distance from which it requires to be seen, a direction viewed from which it vouchsafes most of itself: at a shorter or greater distance we have merely a perception blurred through excess or deficiency. We

8. Maurice Merleau-Ponty, "Cézanne's Doubt," in *Sense and Non-Sense*, trans. H. L. Dreyfus and P. Dreyfus (Evanston: Northwestern University Press, 1964), 14–15.
9. Ibid., *Phenomenology of Perception*, 261.

therefore tend towards the maximum of visibility, and seek a better focus as with a microscope."[10]

In an art gallery, we, indeed, notice our being drawn towards equilibrium, because paintings are special cases in that we have to experiment with each one to find the best grip, and so we oscillate around the optimum, whereas, as experts in perception, in perceiving ordinary objects, we normally are drawn directly to the optimal viewing position.

In either case, as embodied beings, we have to face what we are looking at, move to an appropriate distance given the size of the object, and assure an unencumbered line of sight on it. In this way, our skill takes account of the fact that, as the causal theory of perception makes clear, in order to see an object, we have to be in a position to be causally acted on by the light from it. Thus, from the start, our perceptual skill spontaneously takes account of physical constraint in putting us in contact with physical reality. Indeed, we are so skilled at getting an optimal take on our object that we normally overlook the fact that we have to learn to align ourselves with the constraints of nature in order to perceive at all. Only if some disturbance leads us to recalibrate or move to a new position can we see that the holistic activity involved in arriving at maximal grip bridges the gap between the causal influence of meaningless nature and our meaningful perceptual experience.

All the above skills work invisibly to give all embodied agents access to a world of objects, so, if we challenge Johnny as to why he claims the picture is crooked, he will no doubt say that he just saw it. But, if we persist in asking why he thinks his sight of it was reliable, he might well begin to reveal his epistemological skills. He could point out that the overall illumination was good, he had a viewing position where there was nothing in the way, and he was just close enough to see the details of the picture without losing sight of the whole. And, under those optimal conditions, it looked crooked.

Of course, one could still protest that the picture's *looking* crooked "motivated" Johnny's belief that it *was* crooked but it did not justify it. That is, as in the case of the moon illusion dear to Merleau-Ponty, Johnny may have been led to see what looked like a crooked picture, but, just as we don't believe the moon is bigger on the horizon than at the zenith just because we see it that way, Johnny may not have been justified in forming

---

10. Ibid., 315–316.

a belief just on the basis of how the picture looks. But Johnny has other skills for checking whether the walls and floor are perpendicular, and whatever else may be relevant, and when all the relevant epistemological skills have been utilized to check out all the relevant sources of illusion, he has the right to accede to the belief he has formed, and to conclude that the picture is, indeed, askew.

The moral is that in perception the causal impact of the world does not simply give us beliefs that justify and are justified by other beliefs. Rather, the causal input calls up a complicated set of epistemological skills that produce a stable experience, which, in turn, inclines us to form a belief. Then, if we are cautious or think we are being tricked, we can call on a further set of epistemological skills to check out whether in this case the background is normal. Only then do we have a belief from which we can make reliable inferences that can serve to justify other beliefs.

What is assumed when we give the order is that Johnny knows, as most of us do, how to form a reliable view of this kind of matter. He knows how to go and stand at the right distance and in the right orientation, to get what Merleau-Ponty calls maximum prise on the object. What justifies Johnny's belief, if ever you should want to challenge him on it, is his knowing how to do this, his being able to deal with objects in this way, which is, of course, inseparable from the other ways he is able to use them, manipulate them, get around among them, etc. When he goes and checks he uses this multiple ability to cope; his sense of his ability to cope gives him confidence in his judgement as he reports it to us—and rightly so, if he is competent. About some things he isn't competent (e.g., "Is the picture a Renoir?"), but about this he is.

This shows how in certain contexts we can make perfectly good sense of checking our beliefs against the facts, without swinging off into absurd scenarios about jumping out of our skins.[11] The Davidson-Rorty truism is false.

It also shows, we hope, how a picture can hold us captive, even when we think we are escaping it. It holds us by enframing our thought, so that the arguments we proffer and accept are conditioned by it; and we don't even notice, because it is in the nature of frames to be invisible as long as we're operating within them.

11. Davidson, "A Coherence Theory."

In one way it may seem supremely unfair to accuse Rorty of "representa-tionalism." Does he not himself inveigh against talking of "representation"? "I do not think that either language or knowledge has anything to do with picturing, representing, or corresponding, and so I see formulating and veri-fying propositions as just a special case of what Taylor calls "dealing" and Dreyfus calls "coping."[12] But this assimilation of propositions to modes of coping begs precisely the question at the heart of the mediational issue and confronts Rorty with a dilemma. Either propositions, as opposed to cop-ing practices, must represent the world and so have content, in which case they are inner in the sense that one can separate their conditions of satisfac-tion from whether these conditions are satisfied, or else propositions such as beliefs don't have content. But then how, according to Rorty, could they provide rational justification for other beliefs?

This is where we want to return to our point that just saying you reject a concept is not necessarily climbing out of the picture which embeds it. You also have to explore and bring to awareness how that picture holds you cap-tive. Just walking away avoids doing this.

If we return to the four-strand description of the mediational tradition that we outlined in Chapter 1, we can see how Rorty, and in another way Davidson, still stand within it. The strands were (1) the "only through" structure, (2) the explicitness of content, (3) which one can't get beyond/behind, and (4) the dualist sorting, of the mental and the physical, the space of reasons and the space of causes . Now both Rorty and Davidson vigor-ously reject (1); while Rorty, and less unambiguously Davidson, subscribe to (4). But where the tradition can really be seen as operative is in their acceptance of (2) and (3). The contents of our grasp on the world are to be understood as explicit beliefs (2), and there is no going behind or beyond these in the space of reasons (3): only beliefs justify beliefs.

But the case of Johnny above shows that we can go beyond and below beliefs in the space of reasons, and understand how our primitive contact with the world as embodied agents enables us to generate reliable beliefs, in the way Johnny did. Engaged coping is indeed where the space of causes and that of reasons come together, in a zone where we are both affected and

12. Richard Rorty, "Charles Taylor on Truth," in *Truth and Progress*, vol. 3 (Cambridge: Cambridge University Press, 1998), 95–96.

active, both impinged on by and making sense of things. We have here a paradigm case of how walking away from the issues keeps us in thrall to the picture we want to escape. We can't think through how knowing agents acquire reliable, justified knowledge of the world. We know on one hand that our beliefs emerge out of a causal contact with the world, and, on the other, that we deploy certain procedures and standards of justification. These two relations with things can be explored, but somehow not related.

Until, that is, one is ready to work through the wrong picture, and come up with an alternative as Heidegger and Merleau-Ponty have done. Only at that point can one see how false one's truisms have been.

Thus Rorty's whole way of coping with foundationalism, realism, anti-realism, and such-like issues, cannot but exacerbate his vulnerability to the kind of capture we have been talking about. Essentially Rorty's view resembles closely certain kinds of relativisms and nonrealisms: justification ultimately must appeal to the way we do things here. If that's different from the way they do things there, there is no arbitration in reason. But Rorty repudiates the (much execrated) titles "relativist" and "nonrealist." He does this essentially by trying to convince us to stop asking the questions, to which these positions and foundationalism are rival answers. There are just different ways of dealing and coping. Vocabularies are tools. "Different vocabularies equip us with beliefs that are more or less use in coping with the environment in various respects."[13]

But the considerations above suggest that one can't just walk away from certain questions. Is the mediational construal or the embedded construal (i.e., Heidegger and Merleau-Ponty) more adequate? We're supposed to be able just to drop this question. Nevertheless, we find that one such construal is controlling our thinking. This is unavoidable, and the embedded view can illuminate why. We in a sense "know" much more than we know. The quote marks used refer to the as-yet-unarticulated sense we have of things. We draw on this, or some distorted theorizing of it, all the time in thinking about the world. We do so not just in doing philosophy, as we saw with the coherence theory above, but in perfectly ordinary attempts to find out about things in the world. The distinctions we draw which Rorty finds no use for—for example, between self-understandings, which

13. Brandom, introduction to *Rorty and His Critics*, xiv.

we can't construe as independent objects, and an independent reality, staying put through all changes in description, as the solar system stayed there, waiting for Kepler—are there embedded in our practice. Kepler didn't treat his ellipses as a new proposal about how the heavenly bodies might understand/comport themselves. The enframing understanding of the whole inquiry was that this was the way they had always been, and that his theory would make sense of all observations past, present, and future. We are not importing some hyped-up, metaphysical overlay of commentary (Kepler had some of that, in his views about the perfect solids, but that's another matter). We are just articulating an essential frame of Kepler's inquiry, what gave it its sense, and without which it would have been conducted quite differently.[14]

Indeed, Rorty draws on just this framework understanding when he tells us that we are causally impinged on by the world. Here is no new discovery, but an articulation of what we all have to know to be functioning human agents. Indeed, it is common ground between all theories in this domain, with the possible exception of some raving idealists. But in virtue of what hidden boundary are we allowed to note this fact but forbidden to go on and describe the way our thought is embedded in our active agency, as Heidegger and Merleau-Ponty do? There should be no bar to our articulating the framework understandings by which we actually make sense of our thought and action.

1

So Rorty's aim, like ours, is to free us from the old mediational epistemology, which comes down to us from Descartes. But his way of doing this is to walk away from the whole skein of issues about Mind and World (to use McDowell's phrase): how to relate the space of reasons and the space of causes, how thought is embedded in bodily and social action, and the like. We believe, on the contrary, that you can't free yourself from the distorted picture which the old epistemology articulated without working through it, identifying it,

---

14. Charles Taylor, "Rorty and Philosophy," in *Richard Rorty*, ed. Charles B. Guignon and David R. Hiley (Cambridge: Cambridge University Press, 2003), 171–172.

and seeing where it went wrong—the kind of thing which Heidegger and Merleau-Ponty have done.

Who is right? We want to argue that we are. We do so on the grounds that we can't really escape these issues. Our explicit thinking about the world is contextualized and given its sense by an implicit, largely unarticulated background sense of our being in the world. At some level, we are always living some answers to these questions, whether we like it or not.

That is why the mediational picture can still have a hold on our theoretical imagination even though we declare ourselves free of it. This should alert us to the limitations of the strategy of just walking away. But we can also see what is wrong with this when we note that Rorty's dismissal of these questions pushes him to deny things that we can make perfectly good sense of, things which we can't help saying in some form or other, because they articulate the preunderstanding which makes sense of our practices of learning about the world, describing it, and communicating our findings. So we ask each other to check some claim against the facts, as with the order given to Johnny above. And we talk about successive takes on an unchanging reality, as with theories of the heavenly bodies, and we talk about rectifying mistakes, and getting a less distorted view. And as part of all this, we have no good grounds to repudiate the notion of a representation. Lots of simple everyday sentences (but of course, not all, by any means) are meant to communicate the way things are; they give a "picture" of how things stand, and they are correct if the way things really stand corresponds to this picture. If you try to deny us the right to use such expressions, you just have to recur to close substitutes, because they articulate the background understanding which makes sense of our activities of checking, denying, arguing, agreeing, and so on. It is in this common and well-understood sense that many ordinary indicative sentences "represent" what they're about: there are fifteen chairs in this room—well, are there really?—count them (a reliable way of generating a belief, not itself a belief).

Rorty wants us to drop "represent," while he still uses "belief." But the logic of this word has packed into it the same background understanding. What is a belief about? What exactly does A believe about this thing? Is it true? right? We are up to our ears in the logic of representation, even if a fastidious pragmatism won't allow us to use the word. Moreover, once we deny representation, we are incapable of getting the crucial point of the embedded view, that representations can never be the whole story, that they can't suffice to themselves. Now you can't even think this, because the terms are forbidden. But then, lo and behold, the picture still has you captive anyway when you argue for a coherentist view.

Rorty's way of escape from mediationalism is into a kind of night where all views about Mind and World are shrouded in an equal darkness. You can't look and see any more, articulating what we always already "know" at some level, in the fruitful way that Heidegger and Merleau-Ponty have done. This is what gives his theory an oddly a priori air. We aren't allowed to distinguish between different contexts of truth, where different considerations make our claims true. We have to believe that justification is ultimately a matter of how we do things here, and that you can't arbitrate by argument that it's better or worse than how they do things there. This seems to be a blanket doctrine; there is no sense that issues and contexts immensely differ; that beliefs and representations might figure in one situation but not in another; that an arbitration in reason might be very much in place in one context, and not at all in another. For instance, it seems to us very solidly established that the move from Aristotelian to Galilean-Newtonian mechanics was very soundly grounded. Once you've been through the transition, with the anomaly-resolution it entails, you can't rationally go back; that is, you can't return without forgetting some of the things you've learned. There is a supersession here. But to claim an analogous supersession of baroque over Renaissance music would be absurd. Other cases lie in between, and are more complex. But think of the reasons offered against giving women the vote when they were still struggling for it. How many of them could be repeated today with a straight face? Women were supposed to be incapable of political judgment. People could and did believe this when women were still denied political responsibility. But once they have exercised this for a century, the belief just looks bizarre. Much that we now know would have to be forgotten before one could once more assert this.

In a sense, it is a shame that among so many things which Rorty has jettisoned from the narrow, rationalistic tradition of modern philosophy, he has retained that most irritating habit of the a priori, deciding things wholesale on the basis of highly general considerations. Are differences of conceptual scheme arbitrable? (we apologize for using this condemned term). One is supposed to be able to say yes or no on the basis of some highly general features common to all contexts. Whereas if one really broke the thrall of this kind of philosophy, one would see right away that there is no substitute for looking hard at each new context.

2

So in the end, we owe ourselves an account of how reasons and causes relate in our experience of the world. We can perhaps now see better what is needed to resolve the aporia surrounding this relation, and hence escape from the picture.

In order to breach the hard boundary between the spaces of causes and reasons, we need (1) to allow for a kind of understanding which is preconceptual, on the basis of which concepts can be predicated to things—something, in other words, which functions in the space of reasons below concepts. For this, we need (2) to see this understanding as that of an engaged agent, determining the significances (*sens, Sinne*) of things from out of its aims, needs, purposes, desires. These significances arise out of a combination of spontaneity and receptivity, constraint and striving; they are the ways the world must be taken in for a being defined by certain goals or needs to make sense of it. They are thus in one way imposed on us by reality; what happens is a victory or a defeat, success or failure, fulfillment or frustration; we cannot (beyond certain limits) just choose to deny or alter this meaning. But at the same time, this significance is only disclosed through our striving to make sense of our surroundings.

But (3) the original, inescapable locus of this constrained, preconceptual sense-making is our bodily commerce with our world. This is where Merleau-Ponty's contribution, enlarged and developed recently by Todes, has been so crucial. The most primordial and unavoidable significances of things are or are connected to those involved in our bodily existence in the world: that our field is shaped in terms of up or down, near or far, easily accessible or out of reach, graspable, avoidable, and so on.

But (4) our humanity also consists in our ability to decenter ourselves from this original engaged mode—to learn to see things in a disengaged fashion, in universal terms, or from an alien or "higher" point of view. The peculiar form that this takes in Western culture is the attempt to achieve, at least notionally, a "view from nowhere," or to describe things from an "absolute standpoint." Only we have to see that this disengaged mode is in an important sense derivative. The engaged one is prior and pervasive, as we mentioned earlier. We always start off in it, and we always need it as the base from which we from time to time disengage. But we must be clear that the dependency is genetic here and most emphatically *not* conceptual. (See the discussion in Chapter 2.)

A four-step view of this kind can enable us to overcome the Myth of the Given, and get beyond the paradoxical boundary of mediational theories. But it also dissolves the temptations to antirealism. And this particularly in virtue of step (3). If we see that our grasp of things is primordially one of bodily engagement with them, then we can see that we are in contact with the reality which surrounds us at a deeper level than any description or significance attribution we might make of this reality. These descriptions and attributions may be wrong, but what must remain is the world within which the questions arose to which they were the wrong answers, the world that I cannot escape from, because I need it in a host of ways, in the final analysis even to know who I am and what I'm about[15]—even if what I'm about is renouncing the world to go into the desert. My first understanding of reality is not a picture I am forming of it, but the sense given to a continuing transaction with it. I can be confused about it, but its inseparable presence is undeniable. That is why, as Merleau-Ponty puts it, even to frame the denial, I have to have lost touch with what the words really mean.

Steps (3) and (4) are crucial to our views on the issue of realism versus antirealism. But before pursuing this question, we want to fill out the picture of engaged agency we have been sketching in Chapters 2 and 3.

15. See the illuminating discussion in Todes, *Body and World*.

CHAPTER FOUR

Contact Theory: The Place of the Preconceptual

THIS IS WHERE the description of our predicament in Heidegger and Merleau-Ponty, the analyses of being-in-the-world (*Inderweltsein* and *être au monde*), connect to the powerful critique of dualist epistemology mounted by John McDowell.[1] The dualism McDowell attacks, following Sellars, is the sharp demarcation between the space of reasons and the space of causes. The accounts of *Inderweltsein* and *être au monde* also have no place for this boundary. These accounts are meant to explain, as McDowell's argument does, how it can be that the places at which our view is shaped by the world, in perception, are not just causal impingings, but are sites of the persuasive acquisition of belief. These accounts argue that one can never give an adequate account of this mode of persuasive acquisition, if one focuses just on belief formation at the conceptual level.

We contend that we are able to form conceptual beliefs guided by our surroundings because we live in a preconceptual engagement with these

1. John McDowell, *Mind and World* (Cambridge, MA: Harvard University Press, 1993).

surroundings which involves understanding. Transactions in this space are not causal processes among neutral elements, but the sensing of and response to relevance. The very idea of an inner zone with an external boundary can't get started here, because the fact that we are living things in a certain relevance can't be situated "within" the agent; it is in the interaction itself. The understanding and know-how by which I climb the path and continue to know where I am is not "within" me in a kind of picture. That fate awaits it if and when I make the step to map drawing. But now it resides in my negotiating the path. The understanding is in the interaction; it can't be drawn on outside of this, in the absence of the relevant surroundings. To think it can be detached is to construe it on the model of explicit, conceptual, language- or map-based knowledge, which is of course what the whole I/O tradition, from Descartes through Locke to contemporary AI modelers, have been intent on doing. But just that is the move which re-creates the boundary, and makes the process of perceptual knowledge unintelligible.

And yet, for a while our view seemed to be in disagreement with McDowell himself here, because he refuses this idea of a level of our epistemic contact with the world which would lie below the conceptual. McDowell seems to hold that genuine denizens of the space of reasons must be propositional in form;[2] and he states without ambiguity that sites of the acquisition of genuine belief must be shaped by concepts. By contrast, we are claiming that our propositionally formed beliefs can only arise on the basis of a more original, "primordial" (ursprünglich) epistemically fruitful contact with the world, which is prepropositional and in part even preconceptual.

Let's try to get clearer on the (at least apparent) difference between us by rehearsing McDowell's main line of argument in his rich and convincing book. McDowell begins his book by explaining the temptation to resort to the Myth of the Given. We are aware that we justify some of our beliefs with others, or that we arrive at certain beliefs through chains of reasoning from others. But we also hold that these beliefs must "be grounded in a way that relates them to a reality external to thought. . . . Surely there must be such

2. For instance, when he says things like the following: "But we really cannot understand the relations in virtue of which a judgement is warranted except as relations within the space of concepts: relations such as implication or probabilification, which hold between potential exercises of conceptual capacities." Ibid., 7. The "exercises" referred to here surely must be propositional.

grounding if experience is to be the source of knowledge, and more generally, if the bearing of empirical judgements on reality is to be intelligibly in
place in our picture at all."[3]

The Myth of the Given is a response to this worry. The play of justification of beliefs by other beliefs, which otherwise threatens "to degenerate
into a self-contained game," is saved from this fate by "the putatively reas-
suring idea . . . that empirical justifications have an ultimate foundation in
impingements on the conceptual realm from outside."[4]

But this saving idea turns out to be useless. If the foundations are meant
to be "extra-conceptual impingements from the world, the result is a picture
in which constraint from outside is exerted at the outer boundary of the
expanded space of reasons, in what we are committed to depicting as a brute
impact from the exterior." What happens at this boundary "is the result of
an alien force, the causal impact of the world, operating outside the control
of our spontaneity."[5]

In other words, the space of reasons meets at a certain point the space
of causes, but in the form of a causal impact from without. This impact is
meant to contribute to the justification of our beliefs, but by its very nature
it cannot. Causal impact means that in certain environments, we just find
ourselves with certain beliefs, without insight into why they arise in these
surroundings. This is more likely to generate skepticism than to assuage the
original need for solid empirical justification.

McDowell points here to the paradox in the original mediational theory:
The fact that our basic "simple ideas" come through pure causal impingement is what makes them beyond challenge; they are pure Givens. Reasoning has to start from here; there is no choice. But this very fact is what makes
us wonder whether they are any kind of reliable guide to the world beyond
our representations. The mediational tradition breeds skepticism, and beyond that, antirealism, as torrid sunshine breeds flies.

The problem with the Myth of the (Pure) Given is that it doesn't answer
the need out of which it was generated in the first place. But beyond that, it
also sells us short. Our perceptually formed beliefs are not just there as brute

3. Ibid., 5.
4. Ibid., 6.
5. Ibid., 8.

givens. Perception is precisely the activity whereby we have and can acquire
more insight into why we have the beliefs we do. The inclination to apply
some concept in judgement "does not just inexplicably set in. If one does
make a judgement, it is wrung from one by the experience, which serves as
one's reason for the judgement. In a picture in which all there is behind the
judgement is a disposition to make it, the experience itself goes missing."[6]
Here is a phenomenological truth; and it points up something essential in
the logic of the justification of our empirical beliefs: they do not start from
pure givens that we cannot get behind. This was also the message in our argument in Chapter 3, centering on Johnny's checking the picture.[7]

Now reasoning is an exercise of a norm-guided capacity; it is thus an exercise of spontaneity in us, or otherwise put, of freedom. McDowell here en-
dorses Kant. "When Kant describes the understanding as a faculty of spontaneity, that reflects his view of the relation between reason and freedom;
rational necessitation is not just compatible with freedom but constitutive of
it. In a slogan, the space of reasons is the realm of freedom."[8]

Once we see the emptiness of the Myth of the Given, our problem is
somehow to bring this free spontaneity together with constraint. In order
to stop the oscillation between the need for grounding which generates the
Myth of the Given, and the debunking of this myth, which leaves us with the
need unfulfilled, "we need to recognize that experiences themselves are states
or occurrences that inextricably combine receptivity and spontaneity";[9] we
have to be able "to speak of experience as openness to the lay-out of reality.
Experience enables the lay-out of reality itself to exert a rational influence on
what a subject thinks."[10]

In this description of our task, we are entirely in agreement with Mc-
Dowell. We have to show how our perceiving can be both constrained and
free, situated and yet spontaneous and creative. That is what we were trying

6. Ibid., 61.

7. McDowell's argument runs very close to ours here, including his critical treatment
of the same paper by Davidson, even including his citing the same quotations about the
impossibility of getting beyond beliefs, and not being able to jump out of our skins. Ibid.,
lecture I, section 6. For Davidson reference, see *A Coherence Theory*, 307–319.

8. Ibid., 5.

9. Ibid., 24.

10. Ibid., 26.

to do in Chapter 3. And we have come to the conclusion that this guided spontaneity happens inescapably and primordially at a level below the conceptual—that the exercises of conceptual skills draw on epistemic skills at a deeper level, as we saw in the case of Johnny above. If we want to see how constraint and spontaneity come together, we have to find this in perception; here we heartily agree with McDowell. But if we want to find this in perception, we have to bring out how our ability to form beliefs like "the picture is crooked" draws on preconceptual epistemic skills.

In this last conclusion, we seem to come to a break with McDowell. In his critique of Gareth Evans in Lecture III, he firmly rejects the possibility that the space of reasons could include experiences which are "outside the sphere of the conceptual."[11] Evans's theory is not identical with ours, but we too want to aver to experiences of this preconceptual sort. If we look for McDowell's general reason for rejecting this, beyond the particular arguments directed against Evans's version, we discover that they are built into his position from the very opening pages of the book. Already in Lecture I, section 4, after attributing to Kant the thought "that empirical knowledge results from a co-operation between receptivity and spontaneity," he adds the parenthetical sentence: "Here 'spontaneity' can be simply a label for the involvement of conceptual capacities."[12] The rest of the discussion foregrounds "conceptual capacities" or "conceptual contents" as what needs to be combined with receptivity.

Our difference seems to come down to this. We both give a crucial place to spontaneity in our most basic contact with the world. But McDowell doesn't envisage any spontaneity which is not the exercise of concepts, whereas we, following Merleau-Ponty, have been describing precisely such a subconceptual exercise of spontaneity in our original grasp of our world.

This means that the basic holistic arguments, which we both draw from Kant, are transposed by us from their original register into the preconceptual. We pointed out in Chapter 2 that Kant developed the original holistic argument on which all previous deconstructions of mediationalism have drawn. This is the argument against the atomism of the input, which consists in showing that any particulate percept has to be related to the

11. Ibid., 56.
12. Ibid., 9.

world in which it figures, that we have necessarily to relate bits of knowledge (*Erkenntnisse*) to their object (*Gegenstand*). McDowell takes up this same point: "The object of experience is understood as integrated into a wider reality, a reality that is all embraceable in thought but not all available in this experience."[13] But this is understood as being so by virtue of the way our "conceptual capacities" operate, whereas for us, this kind of holism already functions on the level of preconceptual experience, for instance with the skilled footballer on the field.

Our description above of the footballer provides a good example of pre-conceptual spontaneity. Kant and McDowell speak of "spontaneity," because they see the knowing agent not just passively receiving impressions from the outside world, but actively construing his or her surroundings, making sense of them. This we certainly do by applying concepts much of the time. But clearly not all the time. The footballer is actively "making sense" of the field before him, articulating it into sectors, impregnable zones, possible "open-ings" between adversaries, vectors of vulnerability where the other team can break through; in Gibson's language he is grasping the affordances—all without benefit of concepts. (But the terms we've applied here are ours, not drawn from Gibson's vocabulary.)

Kantian spontaneity is "rational," because it is not just arbitrary, but is directed to making sense of our world, to getting it right. That is why, at the higher levels where we deal with moral issues, we can speak of "free-dom" and say, with McDowell, "rational necessitation is not just com-patible with freedom but constitutive of it."[14] Spontaneity at all levels is guided by the goal of getting it right; being clearly "forced" to come to some conclusion is not its negation, but its highest fulfillment. The same intrinsic relation between spontaneity and necessity that we see in the Kantian moral sage, and the Polanyian scientist,[15] is visible in the unre-flective football player. He too is straining every faculty to get an accurate take on the ever-changing lines of force in the field. But the medium here is not moral reflection or theoretical representation, but the behavioral af-fordances of attack and defense.

13. Ibid., 32.
14. Ibid., 5.
15. Michael Polanyi, *Personal Knowledge* (Chicago: University of Chicago Press, 1958).

That our spontaneity can be preconceptual when we're playing football, but not when we're morally deliberating or weighing theories, has to do with the place of language in our lives—an issue which we will come to later.

So who is right about spontaneity, McDowell or ourselves? Perhaps we both are, and some finer distinctions can reconcile our positions. We heartily endorse McDowell's goal of showing how the space of reasons relates to the space of causes, how spontaneity can be guided, and how causal impingement can be woven into active construal. Indeed, we showed in Chapter 3 how from the start, our perceptual skill spontaneously takes account of physical constraint in putting us in contract with physical reality—a basic fact about perception that Davidson emphasizes but thinks is outside experience. McDowell holds, counter to Davidson, that we must actually experience this causal constraint because otherwise our perception would not connect up with the world, but his account of perception as conceptual all the way out seems to leave no place for the way the causal contact is actually taken up by our perceptual skill. For this happens first of all and inescapably at the preconceptual level; it is something we share with our mute animal cousins.[16]

But perhaps we might also fruitfully ask here: Whence comes the temptation to claim that everything we learn from perception must have propositional form, that the deeper level we are proposing cannot exist?

Perhaps it arises partly from the sense that a "space of reasons" must be a space of reasoning, by which we mean the reflective-critical activity which we carry on when we weigh different propositions, adduce reasons for them, consider alternatives to them, or deduce consequences from them. Clearly these activities require propositionally formulated candidates for knowledge, and it requires the development of prose description of a kind which permits metalevel description and evaluation: Does q follow from p? Are r and s incompatible? And the like. But can we really let reasoning hog the whole

---

16. Here lies, of course, another zone of argument between us. McDowell is naturally forced to see a deep difference between the way we on one hand and animals on the other have "perceptual sensitivity to features of the environment. We can say that there are two species of that, one permeated by spontaneity and another independent of it" (ibid., 69; see also 64). In a sense this is true; acceding to the linguistic dimension (as we explain below) changes the whole game. But our way of conceiving this can allow for a substantial overlap, which seems undeniable.

space of reasons, when it can only get going on the basis of formed beliefs, which in turn always rely, directly or indirectly, on more primitive epistemic skills, such as those exercised by Johnny above?

More fundamentally, we should probe the question: What do we mean by "conceptual" and "preconceptual" in the context of this debate? These terms are far from having a totally fixed meaning in our language, even among philosophers. Do animals have concepts? We might be tempted to say "yes," because after all my dog can recognize bones, and also his dog-house; he can recognize policemen and dog catchers (he bares his teeth and growls fiercely), and me, his master (he rushes up and wags his tail). There is clearly something analogous in this behavior with our ability to recognize cars, and our car, policemen (I nervously check if my seat belt is fastened), and family members.

There is no one place where we have to draw the line here. But clearly McDowell in refusing the suggestion that we have preconceptual experience is thinking of the role of concepts in what we have called reasoning. "It is essential to conceptual capacities, in the demanding sense, that they can be exploited in active thinking, thinking that is open to reflection about its own rational credentials. When we say the content of experience is conceptual, that is what we mean by 'conceptual'."[17] Now presumably my dog doesn't reflect on the rational credentials of his bone-identifications, and so there is undoubtedly a distinction here. We could find another term for it (maybe "conceptual in the demanding sense"?), but let's just follow McDowell's usage and say "conceptual."

But in that case, we should introduce another term to describe what my dog can do, and what we do as football players and as skilled drivers. Let's use "protoconceptual." My dog in chasing the cat up the tree is relying on protoconcepts, because he's not just responding to his environment the way a sunflower does in orienting to the sun. On the contrary his action flexibly tracks the cat as prey, even anticipating some of its moves. But at the same time, his grasp of this world involves protoconcepts, because there is no question of his reflecting critically on the categories he is relying on.

Now it seems clear that active critical thinking, the use of concepts in the full, demanding sense, requires language. We could argue, following Herder

---

17. Ibid., 47.

and others, that the introduction of language puts us in a "reflective" stance to the things we talk about. "Reflective" here has the following sense: when we recognize something by calling it a bone, as against just responding appropriately to bones (as Rover does), we are using a term which could be right or wrong. It is an essential feature of language users that they are sensitive to this issue of correct usage. Of a being, like a parrot, to whom we can attribute no such sensitivity, we would never say that it was describing anything, no matter how unerringly it squawked out the "right word." Of course, as we prattle on, we are rarely focusing on the issue of rightness; we only do so when we get uncertain and are plumbing unexplored depths of vocabulary. But we are being continuously responsive to rightness, and that is why we always recognize the relevance of a challenge that we have misspoken. It's this nonfocal responsiveness which we're trying to capture with the word "sensitivity."

This nonfocal sensitivity is made explicit and central when we take the second-order stance, and ask whether the terms in which we've been recognizing/describing things are correct or not, that is, when we reflect on the "rational credentials" of our thought hitherto. In other words, the Herderian "reflective" stance, essential to language, is at the heart of what McDowell calls "conceptual capacities." We might be able therefore to explore the issue which divides us from McDowell if we look at the place of language in our everyday experience. We'll return to this in section 2.

1

But it still seems unclear where the difference lies. We seem to be talking past each other. In his reply to Dreyfus, after the long and interesting discussion between the two, which has recently culminated in a collection of comments on the debate,[18] McDowell rejects the view that he has no place for the kind of absorbed coping that we consider a paradigm case of the preconceptual. On the contrary, he protests that Dreyfus seems to be assuming that concepts are only in play when we stand back, take a distance, and reflect on

---

18. See Joseph K. Schear, ed., *Mind, Reason, and Being-in-the-World: The McDowell-Dreyfus Debate* (Abingdon, Oxon: Routledge, 2013).

what we are doing. But this, he protests, is not the case. He fully accepts the phenomenon of absorbed coping; only he sees this too (in human beings, not in nonrational animals) as an exercise of conceptual capacities. And he sees Dreyfus as the victim of "the myth of the Mind as Detached," the view that conceptual thinking can only occur in a detached stance.[19]

We might think that this is just a case of our drawing the boundary of the concept "concept" at different places, the possibility we evoked at the end of the previous section. This would make the issue one of arbitrary semantics. But there is more here than that. McDowell seems to accept something like our notion of a protoconcept in talking about the behavior of nonrational animals. But he wants to insist that any human action, however similar it might appear to some form of animal behavior, is conceptual.

We manifest conceptual agency, he believes, because even in cases of the most totally absorbed coping—say, the chess master involved in the match, or the builder hammering a nail—we can give an answer if asked: "What are you doing?" or "Why are you doing that?" Maybe the answer will be rather minimal, and of course we have to break the flow of the action to give it, but the answer (couched in concepts of action or reasons) shows what was conceptual all along.

But McDowell allows that in some cases, people might not have an answer. He takes up the example, often cited by Dreyfus,[20] of people's instinctive sense of how close to stand to an interlocutor in a conversation. The distance can vary with the intimacy or formality of the conversation; and the whole gamut of distances and the predicaments which they are appropriate to will vary from culture to culture. But there is some sense of the appropriate here, which people respond to by stepping back (when the interlocutor insensitively approaches), or leaning forward (at a moment of greater intimacy).

Let's say that my interlocutor steps back in the middle of a conversation, and I ask him: "Why did you do that?" Perhaps this is a provocative question, because I feel rebuffed, seeing him as refusing the intimacy I was assuming between us; but it could also be a question out of genuine puzzlement. And

19. See "The Myth of the Mind as Detached," in ibid, 41–58.

20. For example, see Hubert Dreyfus, "The Primacy of Phenomenology over Logical Analysis," *Philosophical Topics* 27, no. 2 (2000): 3–24.

let's say he replies: "Was I doing that?"[21] Here too, different things may be going on: maybe he is aware of the rebuff, and is trying to cover up to avoid embarrassment; but it may be that here too he is unaware of this, and really didn't notice that he was doing anything—he just stepped back. For McDowell this kind of case poses no problem for his thesis of the pervasiveness of conceptual agency, because this shows that the move in question wasn't an action at all, and so constitutes no counterexample to the pervasiveness thesis, in the meaning of the act.

But this seems to us too easy a way out. Some people might be genuinely unaware of what they're doing here. But this behavior has to be seen as norm-governed, governed by a sense of appropriateness. If some people are really unaware of this, they can be made aware if others point it out to them. Does this whole range of behavior only become action when the agents come to see what they're doing? This doesn't seem right; the behavior is guided by the same considerations before and after.

But this example may suggest what underlies the cross-purposes here. Actions have several descriptions. Under one we may be aware of what we are doing, under others not. The person who steps back is unlikely to be completely sincere if he replies: "Was I doing that?" Minimally, he felt some discomfort, and he stepped back to relieve that. But he did perhaps have no idea of the whole range of appropriate distances which governs our behavior in this culture. And as for me who provoked this move, I was probably very insensitive. If my interlocutor comes right out and says, "You were making me feel uncomfortable," I might try to justify myself afterwards by saying, "But I was behaving correctly, showing interest without being importunate," thus densely refusing to admit awareness of the complex normativity of distance-standing that I had infringed.

We can not only be differentially aware of our actions under different descriptions, but we can also extend (or in cases of desensitization, contract) our awareness to take in levels hitherto unsuspected. Typically, we often do X in doing Y; at time t, we are only able to avow X, but with expanded awareness, we come to a fuller grasp of our agency, incorporating Y. Could

21. McDowell's formulation of the reply is: "Oh did I? I wasn't aware of doing that." *Mind and World*, 13.

this distinction of levels help to resolve the differences between McDowell's and our takes on absorbed coping?

Before examining this, let's look at another example, taken from Dreyfus's contribution to the recent volume on the McDowell-Dreyfus debate.[22] The example, drawn from Heidegger, describes the badly placed chalkboard he is writing on as he lectures.[23]

To begin with, like McDowell, Heidegger notes, and then sets aside, traditional desituated conceptuality: "As an example of a simple assertion we shall take the statement 'The board is black'. [But] we can sense straightaway that this statement is, as it were, ready-made for logic and the study of grammar."[24] So he takes instead as his paradigm an assertion made by an involved coper: "'The board is badly positioned,' is simpler in the sense of something spoken naturally and spontaneously."[25]

Then Heidegger begins to lay out an account of the experience of what, in *Being and Time,* he calls the unready-to-hand: "The position is bad for those who are sitting at the other side of the lecture room or bad . . . for the one who is writing and has to go over to the board each time rather than having it more favorably situated behind him. Accordingly, the position is not a determinacy of the board itself, such as its black color, . . . but a determinacy that is merely relative to us who are here in this very situation. This determinate quality of the board—its bad position—is therefore not a so-called objective property, but is relative to the subject."[26]

But this account, which would presumably fit into McDowell's world of facts and judgements about them, is still too traditional for Heidegger. As if objecting to McDowell's view, Heidegger continues: "[But] the board is

22. Hubert Dreyfus, "The Myth of the Pervasiveness of the Mental," in Schear, ed., *Mind, Reason, and Being-in-the-World,* 15–40.

23. To avoid misunderstanding at this crucial point, it is important to bear in mind that what we have been calling skillful coping, Heidegger calls "understanding." He says, "In ordinary language, we . . . say 'He understands how to handle men,' 'He knows how to talk.' Understanding here means 'knowing how' [*können*], 'being capable of.'" Martin Heidegger, *History of the Concept of Time,* trans. Theodore Kisiel (Bloomington: Indiana University Press, 1985), 298.

24. Martin Heidegger, *The Fundamental Concepts of Metaphysics: World, Finitude, Solitude,* trans. William McNeill and Nicholas Walker (Bloomington: Indiana University Press, 1995), 343.

25. Ibid.

26. Ibid., 344.

not—as this rash interpretation concluded—badly positioned in relation to us who are factically to be found here, rather the board is badly positioned in this lecture room. [If] we think of the room not as tiered, but as a dance hall, then the board would be sitting quite favorably in the corner, out of the way."[27]

And Heidegger then introduces the skilled familiarity in which we live— a familiarity that, in order to function, must remain in the background: "It is out of the manifestness of the lecture room that we experience the bad position of the board in the first place. Precisely this manifestness of the lecture room within which the board is badly positioned is what does not explicitly appear at all in the assertion. We do not first attain the manifestness of the lecture room via the assertion 'The board is badly positioned,' rather this manifestness is the condition of the possibility of the board in general being something we can make judgments about."[28]

The manifestness of the lecture room as a meaningful miniworld is the cumulative skill we have built up through our attending and giving lectures over the years. It is this know-how that orients us in the lecture room and enables us to deal with the things in it. In Heidegger's example, the manifestness of the lecture room is the condition of the possibility of making propositional judgements about the position of the blackboard. The ongoing background coping makes possible the judgement that the blackboard is badly placed. And Heidegger goes on to point out that this background familiarity is holistic and nonpropositional: "What is decisive in this interpretation of assertion is that we do not make a judgment in relation to an isolated object, but in this judgment we speak out of this whole that we have already experienced and are familiar with, and which we call the lecture room."[29] The whole of forces we are absorbed in when we make the judgement that the blackboard is badly placed is not made up of propositional structures to which we can affix bits of language.

Heidegger stresses the nonconceptuality of this holistic background know-how he calls understanding: "Precisely in order to experience what and how beings in each case are in themselves as the beings that they are, we must—although not conceptually—already understand something like the what-being and that-being of beings."[30]

27. Ibid.
28. Ibid., 345.
29. Ibid., 347.
30. Ibid., 357.

The background condition of the possibility of making judgements that such and such is the case, then, must be already pervasively operative. In that, McDowell and Heidegger would agree. But they differ as to what these a priori conditions consist in for a judgement like "the board is badly positioned" and what they reveal. For McDowell making judgements requires operative concepts that correspond to a propositionally structured totality of facts. For Heidegger what is required are nonconceptual coping skills that disclose a space in which things can then be encountered as what and how they are. In disclosing a holistic background by orienting ourselves in it we are not subjects striving to get it right about an independent objective reality, but rather we are absorbed into a field of forces drawing us to keep up our ongoing coping like a pilot staying on the beam. Since there is no mind-world distance in such activity, there is no need for conceptual content to mediate a mind-world relation.

Aligned to our previous example of distance standing, we might say that here someone might be aware that the board is badly positioned. I might be moving the board, and you might ask me why, and that's what I would say. But I would not yet be able to articulate all the deeper reasons that Heidegger cites, which are part of the sense of things which belong to my coping skills as a teacher. Grasping them is an essential constituent in my know-how. I have not yet articulated the concepts, as Heidegger has done in this passage, which could explain the rationale here. On one level, my action in moving the board is done for a conceptualized reason (it's badly placed); on another I am responding preconceptually to this meaningful miniworld.

This way of posing the issue between us ensures that there is a place for the preconceptual, because there are almost always levels of our action where we are responding to nonarticulated features. As we do X through doing Y, it is not always possible to articulate Y; and even if it is, focusing on this may disrupt the flow of X.

2

Thus it seems clear to us that there is an important place for what we might call the prereflexive in our everyday world, in the kind of everyday grasp of our surroundings, establishing an equilibrium with them, which we described in Chapter 3, following Merleau-Ponty. We can in fact see a place for two modes of such prereflexive understandings: the prelinguistic, on one hand, and the prepropositional on the other.

Take the prelinguistic. Of course, much of our human world is already linguistically articulated. We move among chairs and tables, outdoors, into cars, towards buildings or laboratories. But it is never completely so, in the sense that the range of articulacy can be extended. As a boy I go with my dog every day to explore the woods yonder. We have to cross a stream, and we both hop across on some conveniently placed rocks. I don't have a word for these; I don't even feel the need for one. We just both hop across on our way to the inviting, mysterious woods. Then my older cousin comes to visit, sees the woods and the stream, wants to cross, and asks me if there are any "stepping stones." Because "stone" and "step" are already in my vocabulary, I get at once his meaning. But more, I can answer his question, because I recognize at once that this is the right term for those rocks in the river that help me across. These hitherto mute facilitators have entered the linguistic dimension for me thanks to my cousin. They enter this dimension in this immediate and unproblematic way, because I already have some understanding of them, that involved in my skillful use of them as supports when I cross.[31]

So I answer my cousin right away with a "yes." This monosyllable here carries the force of my asserting in another context: "There are stepping stones across this stream." I have a propositionally formed belief, ready to figure in reasonings: for instance, I could justify crossing on the stones by saying: "So we can get to the other side without getting wet and being bawled out by Auntie." But my way to this belief was prepared by a prearticulate, prelinguistic understanding. In the course of this exchange with my cousin, something was transferred out of the prereflexive into the linguistic dimension.

The transfer means that these stones figure in my life in a new way. They were before among the things that I rushed past on my way to my defined goals; I was barely aware of them. They can now figure centrally in a common deliberation with my cousin, in our search for exciting adventure without the penalty of adult disapproval. This is the change that language brings about here.

31. For a further discussion of the linguistic dimension, see Charles Taylor, "The Importance of Herder," in *Philosophical Arguments* (Cambridge, MA: Harvard University Press, 1995), chapter 5.

Now let's look at the prepropositional. Go back to our world of chairs, tables, doors, cars, buildings. I am rushing through this on my way to work, entirely absorbed in the problem I have to face there, perhaps some point of philosophy, perhaps how I am going to deal with the dean who's on my case for my unauthorized trip to a conference. In the meantime, I am skillfully driving, avoiding pedestrians, other cars, lampposts, etc. In a way, these figure in my world almost as the stepping stones do above for the boy prior to the arrival of the more linguistically advanced cousin. I am not at all focusing on them; I am just skillfully avoiding them, as he was skillfully jumping on and off his rocks. The difference is that they already have familiar names; they figure in my articulated world.

But they are still figuring prereflexively. Because here things are just floating by; I am skillfully coping with them, but I am not making any judgements about them.

Here too, as in the skillful coping of the boy crossing the stream, but in a different way, what floats by may be the basis of a later judgement. When I get to the office, I am informed that a dangerous maniac is about. He is driving a yellow Mercedes. Did I see one? I suddenly realize, yes, I did. I saw a yellow Mercedes (or an oddly shaped yellow car that must have been a Mercedes) five minutes ago on Green Street. Now I've formulated a proposition, and framed a new belief about the world: There was a yellow Mercedes at five to nine on Green Street. I am ready to impart this to the police, and they will do all sorts of reasonings with it, and hopefully catch the maniac before further harm accrues. But the capacity to form this useful belief draws on my familiarity with Green Street, gained as I passed through it, not framing propositions, nor forming beliefs about it at all, but rather about the dean as a sanctimonious idiot, etc.

So the beliefs which figure in our reasonings are indeed judgements or propositions, applying concepts. But what we frequently draw on to frame these are understandings or modes of familiarity with our world which are prereflexive, either in the sense of being prelinguistic, or in that of being as yet not judgements or propositions. In the first case (boy jumping on rocks), we didn't at first have a word or concept at all; in the second (driving to the meeting with the dean), we had one in our repertory, but it wasn't serving to make a judgement; we weren't yet officially recognizing this object under this concept, framing a belief about it. But in both cases, we were taking something in, acquiring understanding or familiarity which will later serve as the source of beliefs.

But the way in which and the extent to which the prereflexive experience is such a source is different. In the latter, prepropositional, case, we can say afterwards what we saw, as I said there was a yellow car on Green Street, without needing the prompting of new vocabulary, as in the stepping-stone scenario. In this respect it is analogous to McDowell's case of the absorbed coper, say the chess master, who can explain straight off after the fact why he moved the bishop. This kind of prereflexivity fits McDowell's account, but the first doesn't. Here the earlier experience only facilitates later judgement with the aid of a further act of articulation.

We can see now how perception can feed belief. It can do so because it involves more than belief. It draws on epistemic skills and understandings which operate below the level of belief formation, and frequently operate independently of it. In Johnny's case, they operate together, because he draws on these skills precisely to form a belief about the picture, which is the task we set him. But with the boy on the rocks, and the aggrieved man driving to the dean, we see the skills functioning independently, while still being of later service in framing beliefs.

Where do we differ from McDowell? It's not entirely clear to us what in the above paragraphs he would reject. Certainly we agree with him that after infancy, we humans are always in the linguistic dimension; we may not have words for this or that (the boy crossing the stream on the rocks), or we may not be focally aware of many of the things we have already named, but we can always coin new words, or retrieve focal awareness ex post. We are capable in principle (bar psychic blockages, and given the training) of bringing all our experience under critical scrutiny. And this clearly differentiates us from animals. Even when our actions seem most similar, there are crucial differences. Take the footballer sensing the affordances in a line of defensemen that he needs to break through, and the fox seeking a line of escape from the advancing dogs. For the footballer, one of the crucial constraining features he is responding to is that white line around the field, beyond which the ball will be out of play. A norm here is operating together with the lunging of his opponents to constitute the field he has to navigate. There is nothing analogous in the world of the fox.[32]

32. We owe this example to Terry Pinkard (private conversation).

Nevertheless, we cannot ignore the difference between the prelinguistic and the world already disclosed in language, between the objects of our focal judgements and their tacit surroundings, if only because to do so would be to miss, or even distort, a crucial feature of our experience.

Even our focal judgements, like "the painting hangs crooked," rely on the skillful navigation of affordances, bringing the painting and room into the equilibrium of optimum grasp, for which we have no words (or didn't until Merleau-Ponty and Todes explored this for us). In this ultimate dependence on the preconceptual lies our kinship with the other animals, not endowed with *logos* (which we can translate as either "language" or "reason").

3

Drawing on our account of various prelinguistic, unnoticed, and explicit perceptual skills in the course of this chapter, we can now lay out the full eleven stages of skillful perception and action involved in starting with a causal contract with the physical world and arriving at a justified belief. Needless to say, these stages are usually not discriminated by the agent. Indeed, in some cases, the distinction is notional rather than successive, for example that between 2 and 3 and, sometimes, 5 and 6. It is usually only in cases of breakdown, or of exceptional difficulty, when an ongoing activity is "slowed down," that the distinction between them comes to light.[33]

1. The perceiver (animal or human) is drawn to an optimal position to receive the causal impact of the things in the physical universe, be they distant stars or nearby rocks.
2. The body schema, our prelinguistic and preconceptual familiarity with the world, interacts with the resulting indeterminate experience and segments it into figure and ground.

33. Of course, this is something of an abstraction, because we are starting with a monological subject—in this respect the Johnny case in Chapter 3 was much more typical: it arises out of an *exchange*; Johnny is told to go and check the picture. But in this we are responding to the highly monological way in which these issues are debated because of the bent of the epistemological tradition. We shall raise this issue explicitly in Chapter 6.

3. The visual field as a whole balances various lines of force, settles into a level of background illumination, and maintains its brightness, and color, constancy.

4. The perceiver is simultaneously drawn to move so as to get an optimal grip on the object or objects that are salient in the visual field. They are then experienced as being a certain distance away, and as having a size, shape, orientation, color, etc.

5. Such stable objects can then be relied on and are correlated with a readiness to act on the part of the perceiver. Without language, and without necessarily paying attention, the agent is set to use a stone as affording support, a house as affording entry, and so forth.

6. Given a specific readiness, certain aspects of the perceived object become salient. What stands out is not the color of the stone but its solidity, not the windows of the house but its door, and the agent responds out of sensitivity to such features, still without requiring language. (Since some such responses are appropriate and others turn out to fail, this readiness to act, although prelinguistic, can be thought of as a protobelief, and the resulting action, as a protojudgment.)[34] It goes without saying that something similar takes place with higher animals, such as primates.

7. If the agent is in the semantic dimension, the salient aspects of the object or situation can be articulated linguistically and brought under a concept.

8. The creek crosser can identify the stone as a support; the visitor can identify the door as an entrance. But such conceptual seeing-as can remain prepropositional.

9. Once conceptualized, however, such seeing-as motivates the formation of a belief—in our example, that the stone is a support or that the door is an entrance.

10. Given the successful execution of the above epistemological skills, the belief is normally taken to be reliable.

11. If it is acted upon, and the body-set that gave rise to the belief receives the response it anticipated from the world, the belief is normally taken to be justified.

---

34. Todes, *Body and World*.

The resistance to allowing this preconceptual level, which alone can link the space of reasons to the space of causes, comes partly from the hold of the mediational picture; but it can also come from the related enframing picture of language, which together with the (in our day) growing conviction that language is essential to thought, seems to leave no space for a taking in of information, knowledge, and understanding about the world which could be preconceptual. Only a move to the constitutive picture can allow for a coherent account relating perception and action, understanding, language and belief.

CHAPTER FIVE

Embodied Understanding

SO THE ALTERNATIVE PICTURE which emerges once we deconstruct the mediational one, through a consistent following through of the metacritical turn, is of an embodied agent, embedded in a society, and at grips with the world. The idea is not just that these happen to be facts about the knowing agent which have no relevance to the nature of his knowledge or how it arises. On the contrary; to say for instance that we are embodied is not to say at all the same thing as mechanistic reductivists, who might purport to explain thinking in terms of neurophysiological functioning, for example in terms of computations supposedly realized in the "hardware" of the brain and nervous system. This would leave the nature of knowledge, as construed by the mediational picture, unchallenged. It would still consist in sentences held true, for instance, or their "realizations" in the brain; and these sentences would relate ultimately to a universe of neutral fact, and not human meanings.

But when we say that, for instance, Heidegger, Wittgenstein, and Merleau-Ponty had to struggle to recover an understanding of the agent as engaged, as embedded in a culture, a form of life, a "world" of involvements, ultimately to understand him or her as embodied, we mean something quite different from the above. What does "engagement" mean here? It is to say something like: the world of the agent is shaped by his or her form of life, or history, or bodily existence. We will expand further on this point in Chapter 6.

Our claim about the picture which held us captive is that the dominant mediationalist view has screened out this engagement, has given us a model of ourselves as disengaged thinkers. In speaking of the "dominant" view we are not only thinking of the theories which have been preeminent in modern philosophy, but also of an outlook which has to some extent colonized the common sense of our civilization. This offers us the picture of an agent who in perceiving the world takes in "bits" of information from his or her surroundings, and then "processes" them in some fashion, in order to emerge with the "picture" of the world he or she has; the individual then acts on the basis of this picture to fulfill his or her goals, through a "calculus" of means and ends.

The popularity of this view is part of what makes computer models of the mind so plausible to lay people in our day. These models fit neatly into already established categories. The "information processing" construal builds on a long-supported earlier conception, whereby atomic "ideas" were combined in the mind, and made the basis of a calculation underlying action.[1] Classical Cartesian and empiricist epistemologies provided earlier variants of this conception, which combine an atomism of input with a computational picture of mental function. These two together dictate a third feature: "factual" information is distinguished from its "value," that is, its relevance for our purposes. This separation is dictated by atomism, since the merely "factual" features in order to be computed over must be distinguished from their having some role to play in our goals. But it is also encouraged by another underlying motivation, that of conforming to the protocols of a disengaged natural science, viewing the world from nowhere. In any case, the composite traditional conception has a third feature, which we might call "neutrality," whereby the original input of information is shorn of its evaluative relevance, is merely the registering of "fact."

1. The artificial intelligence researchers turned this rationalist model of thinking and action into a research program. The failure of this program casts serious doubt on this whole scheme. See Hubert Dreyfus, *What Computers Still Can't Do* (Cambridge, MA: MIT Press, 1992).

Now in some respects this view has roots in the common sense of (in any case) our civilization, going back before the modern era. But in other important respects, this conception was shaped and entrenched in modern times by what we've been calling the mediational construal, in particular here by the fourth feature of it enumerated above, which we have called the "dualist sorting." And indeed, this filiation between Cartesian epistemology and modern reductive theories of mind was invoked in Chapter 1.

Now replacing this picture with the engaged or embedded one involves a very profound change. We move away from a mediational picture to a contact one. Our grasp of things is not something which is in us, over against the world; it lies in the way we are in contact with the world, in our being-in-the-world (Heidegger), or being-to-the-world (Merleau-Ponty). That is why a global doubt about the existence of things (does the world exist?), which can seem quite sensible on the representational construal, shows itself up as incoherent once you have really taken the antifoundationalist turn. I can wonder whether some of my ways of dealing with the world distort things for me: my distance perception is skewed, my too great involvement with this issue or group is blinding me to the bigger picture, my obsession with my image is keeping me from seeing what's really important. But all these doubts can only arise against the background of the world as the all-englobing locus of my involvements. I can't seriously doubt this without dissolving the very definition of my original worry which only made sense against this background.[2]

We speak of a contact picture. In what does the contact consist? In the fact that at the most basic, preconceptual level, the understanding I have of the world is not simply one constructed or determined by me. It is a "co-production" of me and the world. That's what it means to say that our grasp of the world at this level is not in us but in the interaction, the interspace of our dealings with things. I take this glass, lift it, drink water from it. The "affordance" it offers me here, to use Gibson's expression, is just one of many features which could be discovered in the glass, and in that sense my take is partial, limited. But partial though it is, it is in another way unshakeable,

---

2. "To ask whether the world is real is not to understand what we are saying" (*Se demander si le monde est réel, ce n'est pas entendre ce que l'on dit*). Maurice Merleau-Ponty, *Phénoménologie de la Perception* (Paris: Gallimard, 1945), 396.

incorrigible. What could a skeptic say here? The only recourse would be the ultimate one of conjecturing that I might be dreaming. How seriously we should take this challenge will depend on our understanding of lived time, as we said in Chapter 1.

But our point here is that the skeptic's recourse is to raise a question whether I am dealing with anything at all, whether this whole sequence is a dream. But less extravagant doubts utterly fall away. Insofar as I am grasping this goblet and drinking from it, it has the "grasp and drink" affordance. That's because this affordance shows up for me in the process of my grasping the glass, in my interaction with this thing. It is not an idea that I have concocted on my own, nor an "impression" in my mind, which may or may not coincide with its distal cause. It is something "coproduced" by me and the goblet, in our interaction.

At the higher, scientific level, we are always dealing with representations of reality which could turn out to be wrong, and part of good scientific method is always to be aware of this. Indeed, any formulated belief may be wrong, even one about such affordances, because we can always misspeak. But at the most primitive level of our grasp of things, there is a contact which straddles the gap between "subject" and "object," and which shows these terms to be ultimately out of place.

There is thus a deep rift between two directions of thought in our time, both of which claim to be deconstructing the traditional epistemology. Some people think that what we really ought to be against is just foundationalism, that is, the attempt to offer a convincing construction of knowledge "from the ground up." They think you can show this to be impossible on Quinean holist grounds, or on grounds closer to older skeptical arguments. But they are willing to leave in place what we're calling mediationalism, that is, an account of the agent's knowledge which is distinct from the world.

For others (here we include ourselves), the exciting thing about deconstructing Cartesianism is the relegation of this picture of the "subject." The idea is deeply wrong that you can give a state description of the agent without any reference to his or her world (or a description of the world qua world without saying a lot about the agent). Such a description would be possible if the knowledge were "in" the "subject." But it isn't; the grasp is in the contact, the interaction, and this interaction can't be described while just talking about the agent.

The belief that you might be able to give a state description of the agent alone might even be taken as a fifth criterial feature of the mediational picture, alongside the four cited above. We might see it as a "fifth dogma of epistemology." But we don't need to multiply the markers of this inadequate picture. It's clear that this fits with the others.

1

We have just summed up our contact or interactive view of the agent in the world. The phenomenological arguments seem compelling. But people very often want to reply to these arguments by saying that they are just phenomenological. They tell us how things appear, but how about how things really are? After all, since Galileo, we are used to the idea that appearances may deceive: the sun is not really sinking below the horizon; of course, the cart stops as soon as we leave off pushing it, but that doesn't mean that all moving objects require a continual application of force to keep going. And so here: of course, there doesn't *appear* to be any mediational element between mind and world. In this respect, modern theories are different from the old empiricism, which seemed to claim that attentive observation reveals that the primary object of consciousness was our "impressions" or "ideas." But these modern theories return on another level with an underlying materialist explanation of experience, in which it all depends on states that are inner in another sense: within the organism, rather than within the mind, but nevertheless separate from the external world.

So where we are inclined to say, for instance, that my ability to get around my hometown, say, doesn't exist in my mind, or even just in my body, but in my active-body-walking-the-streets, an influential contemporary mode of thought would claim that this ability is coded in the brain, and it is something my brain might have, even though it were being kept alive in a vat, without contact with streets or city. This is the kind of view espoused, for instance, by John Searle, who is a strong proponent of the hypotheses that we could have all the conscious experiences we enjoy now, even if we were brains in vats. Indeed, Searle's proof seems to run something like this: after all, we *are* brains in vats—only in our case, the vats are our crania. So why couldn't our actual situation be replaced by the one described in the film *The Matrix*, where the unfortunate humans have their whole organisms confined to vats, and where their brains are fed the kind of input and output correlations which ensure that they will have exactly what is needed to give them the conscious experience of walking around in active, normal life, in a space containing fellow human beings? So that they take a life which in some ways resembles a dream, for real, normal life.

Then, surely, one might object to us, we would not be in real contact with the intentional objects which seem to exist in the Matrix world. All there would be in common with our normal lives would be the similarity in brain states. But if the brain states were exactly the same in both cases, then surely we could say even in the normal case that, given the appropriate input-output connections, our ability to get around was all encoded in our brains.

Note that this reflection fits with one of the standard arguments of the mediational theory, the so-called "argument from illusion." The argument usually goes like this: there are illusions; we think we see a snake, and there is only a rope; we think we see an oasis, and there is only desert there; and so on. Now surely, if we are to be fooled, the subjective visual experience must be exactly the same where there is illusion and where we are truly perceiving. So even the normal case must be made up of a certain kind of inner experience on one hand, and an external object truly corresponding to it on the other. It is this second element which isn't there where we suffer illusion.

The argument forces us to see our normal situation as mediational, as a contact with the world through some inner state. And this is what the brain-in-the-vat scenario does. If the Matrix people could have exactly our experience of normal, waking life, while being inert in vats hooked up to electric impulses, then surely this experience depends on there being these impulses as input, and only mediately on there being real things of the appropriate, believed-in kind out there which produce the impulses, which could also for all we know be generated by the controllers of this domain of vat-confined inert bodies.

The challenge to us by the brain-in-the-vat hypothesis could be framed this way: how can you say that the ability to get around lies in the interspace of body and world, when for all you know there may be no world of the kind you confidently suppose, and where the experience of there being such a world is sufficiently explained by the sequence of states of your brain?

At first blush, it doesn't seem easy to reply to this objection. The hypothesis that we might really in fact be like the denizens of the Matrix is like the extreme skeptical suppositions which have been entertained, for example, by Descartes, that our whole life might be a dream. We could just reply by pointing to our actual experience, noting that there are things that we can do only in interaction with the actual objects in the world: getting from A to B in our hometown, or tying a bow tie. We are incapable of, say, drawing a map, or giving a set of instructions, that is, of generating some kind of representation of what has to be done. Thus I can only help you tie your tie by getting around behind you and tying it on your neck as I do on mine. I can't explain it to you, or draw you a diagram of the movements, or even make the movements in the absence of the tie. Phenomenologically, the ability is in the interspace.

But our opponent would reply: the ability although only exercisable in the execution must rely on some condition of your brain. Of course, in real life, this condition came about through the usual modes of learning, trial and error, or practice under the guidance of a teacher who had a similarly inarticulate grasp of it. But it's quite possible that it could have been induced in some other fashion—for instance, the way Trinity in the film learns to fly a helicopter.

To which we reply: it depends on what you mean by "possible" here. There is a strong and a weak sense of this term. Weakly used, we say something is possible where, as far as we know, there is no obstacle in the way things are to this occurring. Time travel may be judged possible in this sense, because there are many things we do not fully understand about time. But we can easily conceive that it might in fact be impossible, in the stronger sense, that it is ruled out by the way things work in our world.

The brain-in-the-vat hypothesis, that is, the idea that a certain sequence of correlated sensorimotor impulses, however produced, is a sufficient condition of our having conscious experiences of coping with a space-time world just like ours, is clearly possible only in the weak sense. It might turn out that in fact, this couldn't be done.

Let's look at some obvious considerations. We in fact understand very little, one might say almost nothing, about the way in which conscious experiences actually supervene on our bodily states and actions. What guarantees us that the bodily condition on which they supervene is simply a state of the brain, rather than, say, the brain and nervous system, or even the brain in the whole body, or whether they need the active body in its environment? The unruffled certainty enjoyed by people like Searle, that sufficient conditions of conscious experience must be available in the brain alone, is surely a relic of Cartesianism still active in their work—a kind of unconscious a priori they have not yet escaped from.

In fact, recent research on the formation in infants of neural connections to and in the brain indicates that the wiring is shaped by their attempts, eventually successful, to get around in the world, grasp things, see things, get done what they strive to accomplish.[3] It is beginning to look as if the brain-in-the-vat hypothesis is quite out of phase with the way the world of organic beings actually works.

A similar a priori seems to infect what we might see as the template for the brain-in-the-vat hypothesis, the arguments from illusion. As we saw above, these arguments all suppose that in the case of illusion there must always be a subjective experience exactly like that of veridical perception. But is this really so?

Say someone dreamed last night that they had a conversation with Joseph Stalin. A frightening experience; but was it exactly like really visiting the dictator in the Kremlin? Recount the dream sequence: immediately before my conversation, I was at home in Montreal; some way into the conversation my interlocutor morphed into a particularly unpleasant colleague in my department. Viewed in the critical light of waking consciousness, the sequence was very low on verisimilitude. It needed the close, uncritical flow of the dream to make me feel the frisson of encountering the real thing. The illusion depended more on this than on similarity of content with the genuine experience. Similar remarks can be made about some hallucinations, as Merleau-Ponty points out.[4]

In both these arguments and the brain-in-the-vat hypothesis, it is assumed that there is some X—here a state of subjective experience, there a condition of brain firings—which is exactly alike between truth and illusion. But on examination, this is far from necessarily the case. The sense of necessity is an illusion cast by the mediational *Bild.*

We need to set this kind of a priori aside. But nothing forbids a more empirically minded Searle, nudged by his residual Cartesian intuitions, from betting that at the end of the day, research will show the brain-in-the-vat hypothesis to be correct; just as we, impressed by the way that our abilities to cope exist in the interspace of agent in world, are tempted to bet that we need the whole agent-in-world to replicate experience. Our sense is that, in

---

3. See Alva Noë, *Out of Our Heads* (New York: Hill & Wang, 2009).
4. See Merleau-Ponty, *Phénoménologie de la Perception.*

spite of the impressive evidence for the brain basis of experience revealed by current neuroscience, this gives us only the necessary causal conditions; but the sufficient conditions require the agent coping in situation.

So what to think of these hypotheses, in particular of the scenario in *The Matrix*? We have presented a strong phenomenological case for a contact theory, in which we must see ourselves as dealing with the world, such that the locus of our experience and performance cannot simply be identified as inside us. But these scenarios could be seen as presenting a skeptical challenge to our ordinary consciousness. They situate us firmly in an independent world, but perhaps that situation itself is pure appearance, and a purely inwardly generated one at that.

Should this concern us? The view we have been expounding is that we are in contact with the world, wholesale as it were: although we may be wrong about this or that take on things which we have confidently accepted up to now, this error is situated within a general grasp of our situation which cannot be entirely wrong, and which often offers the purchase we need on things in order to correct our views. In a sense, the scenario of *The Matrix* pushes this possibility of regional error to the limit, to the point where it threatens to spill over into the wholesale.

What is limited about the error that the Matrix dwellers suffer from is that they share with the humans once liberated from the vats the same structure of world: we are agents among other agents, in a world which is shared, and which impinges on all of us alike. Moreover, our take on things is as described by John McDowell, as we quoted him in Chapter 4: we see ourselves as open to the layout of reality; we see our take on things as motivated by the reality impinging on us; the causal basis of our perception and the objects of our perception converge. (Of course, "causal basis" here doesn't refer to the kind of purely passive reception dreamt of in classical empiricism. We are always actively construing the world; but we see the upshot of this construal as responding to what is actually there, and in this sense causally dependent on it.) The contrast between real world and Matrix world is that this take on things is right for the former and wrong for the latter. In the Matrix, it seems that our perceiving a car is causally dependent on there really being a car here, whereas in fact it is causally dependent on the programmers feeding certain sensory impulses into our brains.

But maybe this is just a fact about the scenario of this particular movie; suppose the programmers tried to make us live our world as dinosaurs, or mice, for instance. Once again, a weak possibility approaches a boundary where it might very well transgress real possibility. Could someone equipped anatomically and biologically as a human being really see itself as a saurian—at least in anything other than the weak sense that a dream sequence may horrify us with this sense of ourselves? Once again, we lack the knowledge to decide what the limits are here, but it is clear that they may be severe. We could perhaps be induced to dream a saurian fantasy, and in our vat-confined existence, we could never wake up to the critical stance which would reveal this as a fantasy, but that doesn't amount to living something experientially indistinguishable from the real thing.

What can we say about all this? On one level, perhaps this: that *The Matrix* scenario, within plausible limits, would still involve at a certain level a true grasp of what it's like to be in the real world, at least with regard to the structural features of experience. But this might not be thought to be a very meaningful claim, since all the details of the Matricians' lives are false. But of course, it is not clear that even the scenario of *The Matrix* is really possible, as we argued above. And even if it were, we can only conceive of it within a framework which structurally offers the possibility of "waking up" to the real world. Merleau-Ponty's adage, which we have quoted before—"to ask whether the world is real is not to understand what we are saying" (*se demander si le monde est réel, ce n'est pas entendre ce que l'on dit*)[5]—turns out to be right even here, albeit in a sense much weaker than he intended: a world structurally like ours, the world of the programmers, must be there for the scenario to be carried through.

What's the moral of all this? It is clear that brain-in-the-vat, or Matrix, scenarios offer only the most tenuous and implausible objections to our contact theory. And even if it were to turn out that all the processing underlying our relation to the world is in fact done in the *brain*, that wouldn't show that the Cartesian representationalist view of the *mind* was justified. The nonmediational phenomenology, our direct contact with the world, would still stand.

In general, we must resist the Cartesian residue in our thinking that leads us to suppose that the mere fact that brain-processing underlies our relation to the world supports mediationalism, and its attendant global skepticism.

5. Ibid., 396

The fact that there is a causal basis of our experience of the world—whether that basis be in the brain, the body, or in the whole interaction of the embodied agent in situation—does not support a mediational story. Against the grain of the whole Cartesian tradition, it is important to recognize that the underlying causal processes don't stand between us and the world, but are what makes possible our direct contact with it.

And in fact, it appears more and more likely that the sufficient conditions for this direct encounter with reality are to be found in the whole organism-world interaction, as the phenomenology we have presented here suggests.[6] As Michael Wheeler puts it, "In its raw form, the embodied-embedded approach revolves around the thought that cognitive science needs to put cognition back into the brain, the brain back into the body, and the body back in the world."[7]

6. A neurodynamical account of brain activity which would underlie the holistic phenomena we have been describing here, has been worked out by neurophysiologist Walter Freeman. He writes:

> Macroscopic ensembles exist in many materials, at many scales in space and time, ranging from the chemical assemblies within single cells up to ecological networks, social organizations, weather systems such as hurricanes and tornadoes, and even galaxies. In each case, the behaviour of the macroscopic elements or particles is constrained by the embedding ensemble, and microscopic behaviour cannot be understood except with reference to the macroscopic patterns of activity. . . .
>
> Having attained through dendritic and axonal growth a certain density of anatomical connections, the neurons cease to act individually and start participating as part of a group, to which each contributes and from which each accepts direction. . . . The activity level is now determined by the population, not by the individuals. This is the first building block of neurodynamics.

Walter J. Freeman, *How Brains Make Up Their Minds* (Weidenfeld & Nicolson, London: 1999), 55.

7. Michael Wheeler, *Reconstructing the Cognitive World: The Next Step* (Cambridge, MA: MIT Press, 2005), 11.

CHAPTER SIX

Fusing Horizons

IT WOULD HELP here, perhaps, to attempt another summary of the main line of our argument, and in this way to bring out another dimension of the view of human agency we are proposing.

We identified above (Chapter 1) one of the main motivations for the turn to mediational epistemologies, starting with Descartes. This turn is powered by a sense of good critical method. In order to challenge established views, you may have to make what is merely taken as granted explicit; it may be very useful to break some claim down into its component elements, or the separable bits of evidence it relies on; it may be essential to split a merely factual claim from a questionable valuation, or to make a sharp distinction between our take on things and the way they really are.

All this is very true and often crucially important. The basic error was to ontologize this method, to conclude that because this is often the good way to think, it is somehow the way the mind always works, so that we are supposed always to be taking in bits of explicit, neutral information, and combining them. Only we often do this sloppily, inattentively, or too much under the spell of some external authority, and we need to be called back to a more careful, reflective construction.

Against this, our claim has been that in fact our original way of being in the world, coping with reality, finding our way about, reflects a kind of understanding in which none of these distinctions between explicit, analytical elements figure, no more than those between fact and value, or belief and reality. Ontologizing method, reading the explicit, atomic bits of neutral information back into our everyday commerce with the world, not only distorts our everyday reality, but hides from us what an achievement critique is. We fail to see how it requires a shift in our stance to the world, disengaging ourselves from the ordinary meanings of things, decentering ourselves from our involvements in our surroundings.

The Heideggerian term "primordial" (*ursprünglich*) has been used to make this point. Ordinary, engaged coping is primordial, not only because it is in fact our first way of being in the world, which we can never wholly abandon, but also because the decentered, critical stance can only arise from within this ordinary way of being, suspending it completely in relation to our objects of study, but always relying on our everyday coping skills.

Of course, one can understand the motivation for this ontologization. To start with, the whole foundational enterprise is hopeless unless we can dig down to rock-bottom bits of explicit evidence, on which the edifice of science can be reared. This undoubtedly must have weighed with the pioneers of the tradition, like Descartes and Locke. But even after foundationalism is abandoned, the hope for total clarity about human reasoning, and/or for a clear scientific account of it, continues to confer a premium on the atomic and the explicit. We can see this with computer-inspired models of human thinking which have been popular in our age. These too require computation on explicit bits of information, and have no place for the (gestalt) holism of our being in the world. And certain modes of critique base themselves on the (unfounded) belief that factual premises can always be split from evaluative ones in our deliberations.

Now another feature of good method, at least from Descartes' point of view, was that it forced us back onto our own judgement, each to his or her own. We cannot take these matters on authority, but each of us must be assured that the basis of our thinking is really clear and distinct, and that the chains of argument are so as well. There is an animus in this line of thinking against taking things from established tradition, or on external authority. We are called in the end to be "self-responsible" in our critical thought.[1]

This feature of critical method, valid as it often is, has been ontologized, so that it is assumed that the primary subject of knowledge is the individual. And this too has generated an immense distortion of the human condition. We cannot go into the full significance of this here; that would require at least another book. But some aspects of it are directly relevant to our argument.

Once we realize that critique is only possible through a shift in our stance, and once we reflect that shifts of this kind develop and enter our repertory with the evolution of human culture, we see right away that it is a huge and potentially fatal oversimplification to think that critique is simply realized in and by self-responsible individuals. True, it is sometimes the case that one person stands out against an erroneous consensus (and our modern Western culture has tended to celebrate this kind of case); and it may happen that such a heroic figure may even invent a new kind of critique; Socrates, Descartes, and Kant can be seen as examples. But even the most innovative move, which adds something new to our historical repertory of critical stances, doesn't come ex nihilo; it builds on the already established modes; and even the heroic innovator had first to be trained and socialized into these, before striking out on his or her own. How much more do we ordinary followers need to receive the tools of our own critical work from our culture?

These various stances of disengagement or of decentering are developed in language, which shows here as elsewhere a crucial articulative function. Language not only serves to describe what we have already identified and singled out, but can also be used to give expression to new ways of talking, thinking, questioning—and therefore bring them for the first time into our repertory. Socrates is once again a paradigm example, honored in our tradition. We now have (partly thanks to Plato as well) a new word, "dialectic"; but this doesn't serve to describe a preexisting reality; rather this word serves to focus our awareness of a novel kind of questioning exchange, which was

1. The expression is Edmund Husserl's, from a passage in his *Krisis* lectures in which he identifies, across all the differences, with the fundamental stance of Descartes. For Descartes' own attitude to established authorities, see the negative reference to "our desires and preceptors" (*nos appétits et nos précepteurs*) in the *Discours de la Méthode* (Paris: Flammarion, 2000); for Locke's, see the introduction to *Essay Concerning Human Understanding*.

born along with it. Similarly, "idea" comes to be used in a new way by Descartes, with a new technical sense, to designate something which didn't figure in people's self-understandings previously, a basic unit of information, purely in the "mind." Kant also widens our repertory in giving the term "critical" itself a new and specialized meaning.[2]

These great thinkers gave us new concepts; but we shouldn't simply focus on these. It is not just that our repertory of description has been enriched, in the way a good botanist, for instance, can enrich it. What we have been given are new ways of carrying through criticism together. New moves arose within existing forms of conversation, which ended up transforming these conversations. Before Socrates, Athenians certainly argued about what was really just or pious, but the turn to a collaborative but agonistic search for a definition which would not collapse into incoherence was a new (and maddening) mode of continuing the argument, a new direction of inquiry. Against the whole atomist thrust of the mediational position, we have to remember the primacy of the conversation here, both the matrix in which the new move could be made, and the transformed kinds of exchange which it enables and which flow from it.

This point has been made in the last century in a host of ways. Wittgenstein has shown how we cannot grasp the meanings of certain terms unless we see how they figure in the (social) language games they arise in. And these games in turn need to be placed within the whole *Lebensform* they help to constitute.[3] Others have pointed out that in order to understand a given use of a concept, or the sentences in which it figures, we have to identify the genre of discourse in which it occurs. Construal cannot be of single sentences; we need to know the "text" in which they are embedded. And many of the genres of "text" are in fact exchanges, conversations in which, for instance, the reference of the pronouns in one "speech" passes through the referring expression occurring in others.

This foregrounding of the primacy of conversation, of the language games of critique over the individual moves of disengagement or decentering into a critical mode, enriches the understanding of human agency

2. For a further discussion of this expressive-constitutive function of language, see Charles Taylor, "The Importance of Herder," in *Philosophical Arguments* (Cambridge, MA: Harvard University Press, 1995), 79–99.

3. Ludwig Wittgenstein, *Philosophische Untersuchungen*.

which we need to recover from the mediational distortion. In the Heidegerian language invoked above, primordial agency, in its engaged coping, operates within a repertory which is shared; the agent is not first an individual, but one among others, whose joint participation within shared forms is essential—even in establishing that segment of my repertory in which I can come to function alone.

Underlying our explicit, decentered, disengaged, even solitary thinking is a more basic contact with reality, not only with the world with which we are at grips, but also with those others who are at grips with it together with ourselves.

What emerges from the brief discussion in the preceding paragraphs, is that there are two main avenues of refutation of the mediational view, which we outlined at the beginning of Chapter 2. In general, in Chapters 2 to 5, we have been following the first axis of refutation, that which challenges the centrality of mental representations to knowledge. But this leaves untouched the second line of argument, which targets the monological focus of traditional mediational theory. Mediationalism, from Descartes on, as we have just seen, is partly powered by a sense of what good method is; and this method is understood as paradigmatically monological, carried out by and in individual minds. But now it is time to take up the second theme in the above paragraphs, and underline the primacy of conversation in human linguistic life. The methods and forms of critique, the ones we draw on and operate within, are established first in our culture. True, some of us are Socrateses, and help to originate hitherto unknown forms, but these only become part of the heritage of our successors because they are taken up by the culture we bequeath to them.

In Chapter 6 we will be operating clearly on this second track.

1

As we've just noted, a very important area in which we want to distinguish something like scheme and content is where we are dealing with the very different "takes" of very different cultures on nature and the human condition. Here as well, the view we have been defending cannot allow that these differences are insurmountable or inescapable. The embedded view, in fact, offers resources for recognizing differences of scheme, without generating arguments for nonrealism. The conception of the knowing agent at grips with the world opens possibilities quite different from those available on the mediational view. There may be (and obviously are) differences, alternative takes on and construals of reality, which may even be systematic and far-reaching. Some of these will be, all may be, wrong. But any such take or construal is within the context of a basic engagement with/understanding of the world, a contact with it which cannot be broken off short of death. It is impossible to be totally wrong. Even if, after climbing the path, I think myself to be in the wrong field, I have situated myself in the right county, I know the way back home, etc. The reality of contact with the real world is the inescapable fact of human (or animal) life, and can only be imagined away by erroneous philosophical argument. And it is in virtue of this contact with a common world that we always have something to say to each other, something to point to in disputes about reality.

How are we to understand this possibility of communication? We can think of it on two levels. First of all, in virtue of the way we are all as human beings in contact with the world through engaged coping, we share something important. We all have to find our feet within the boundary conditions of the same world, on the basis of the same kind of bodies, basic capacities, and so on. Moreover, we all share the same basic needs: food, clothes, shelter, rest, and the like. This virtually ensures that when we enter a new culture, even with no preparation at all, as when explorers land on a hitherto unknown continent, both sides can start to learn each other's language; they know that everyone will pick out as salient middle-sized moving objects, so they can teach each other the word for "rabbit." They understand that it is useless to point to a rabbit which is obscured from the interlocutor's view by a tree. They know that everyone needs food, so they can request it, barter it, and so on.

This is a level of communication which everyone recognizes, and we are not saying anything here with which our mediational opponents will disagree. But this leaves untouched the most difficult kind of differences. Our first level is the universally human, and is closely linked with our similarity as organic beings—in certain cases, even with what we share with the animals. But the intractable differences which seem to defy understanding are at the level of culture, or of the specifically human meanings, which are disclosed in language. Things we might describe in the following ways: the religion and the rituals of this society seem strange to us, we cannot see why anyone would ever adopt these, they may even be repugnant; or what seems to us their code of honor seems unbalanced: they strain at trivialities and let important things go by; their attitude to death, both their own and that of others, is hard to understand: in our eyes they are too easily willing to inflict death or suffer it; what we might describe as their political system defeats our understanding: they don't seem to have a government at all. As we shall see later, there is a problem with this way of describing the differences, but it can do as a handy fashion of identifying the phenomenon.

Here we are dealing not with what we might call life meanings, which we share as biological creatures, but with meanings on a moral, or an ethical, or a spiritual level, having to do with what are seen as the highest goals, or the best way of life, or moral obligation, or a noble style of being, or virtues of one kind or another. Let's call these "human meanings," because they're the kind of thing we find among humans, as linguistic and cultural beings, and not among the other animals. Of course, these two levels are only notionally separated. In actual human life they are profoundly interwoven, as we shall discuss below.

These human meanings are connected to a point or purpose. And we can fail to see the point. We can perhaps locate it in general terms, as in the above descriptions, where we said that their religion was strange, or their code of honor unbalanced. But this identification doesn't resolve the puzzlement; it just situates it. When my interlocutor flies into a rage at some (to me) anodyne remark, I can't see for the life of me what there is here which damages his honor. The *point d'honneur* here quite escapes me.

Indeed, it can be so opaque that the question arises whether I have located the right general description; maybe it's not a matter of honor at all. More profoundly, maybe this society doesn't have a dimension of concern which corresponds to the term I'm using. Maybe they don't have points of honor. Maybe they don't have a religion, anyway in something like the sense that term has for us. Here we can see why locating what the differences are about can be a far from innocent move, and may quite block further understanding. We will recur to this below.

In any case, on this cultural level, the difficulty is that we are unable at first to see the point of their moral, ethical, or spiritual meanings. And yet we do manage to communicate, at least sometimes. We overcome the barriers and come to see what they're about; whether or not we actually come to want to espouse this way of life or not, we come to understand what is important to them. How is this possible?

Mediationalism frequently has the effect of making us question whether it really is possible, because it suggests that each culture develops its own scheme defining its human meanings, which the members of that culture cannot escape. Where the schemes are different, communication breaks down. Hence the interdict accepted in certain circles on the Left, until recently, on anyone in a hegemonic position trying to articulate the worldview of someone in a subaltern position, whether it be anthropologists explaining the outlook of the society they had studied, or a man explaining the standpoint of women, etc. There always had to be an illegitimate "appropriation of the voice" of the less powerful by the dominant.

Less radically, even if some understanding is allowed, the mediational picture tends to encourage a kind of relativism. The different standpoints are incommensurable, and there is no reality against which they can be judged. So they cannot be ranked. This can, of course, be the basis of a plea for tolerance, and peaceful coexistence.

In this context, one can see the point of an attempt to establish the possibility of universal communication through an outright rejection of the idea of a conceptual scheme, as famously proposed by Donald Davidson,[4] Rorty's espousal of which we were invoking earlier.[5] Davidson means his argument to be taken as a repudiation of the whole representational epistemology. "In giving up the dualism of scheme and world, we do not give up the world, but re-establish unmediated touch with the familiar objects whose antics make our sentences and opinions true and false."[6]

But we think the Davidsonian rejection of the distinction runs us into incoherence or worse. The standard danger here is ethnocentrism, misunderstanding the other because he or she is interpreted as operating with the same classifications as we are. The differences in behavior are then often simply coded as bad versus good.

4. Donald Davidson, "On the Very Idea of a Conceptual Scheme," in *Inquiries into Truth and Interpretation* (Oxford: Clarendon Press, 1984), chapter 13.

5. Rorty, *Philosophy and the Mirror of Nature.*

6. This phrase makes unambiguously clear Davidson's rejection of strand (1) of the composite picture of mediationalism. But the picture hangs on, as we argued above, in the other strands. Donald Davidson, "On the Very Idea," 198.

We believe that a more adequate account of the difference, and how it can be bridged, is found in Gadamer's account of intercultural understanding. "Understanding is always the process of a fusion of horizons supposedly existing for themselves" (*Verstehen [ist] immer der Vorgang der Verschmelzung . . . vermeintlich für sich seiender Horizonte*).[7]

Gadamer's concept "horizon" is something like our notion of "background"; it designates the surrounding context within which the particular things we do, say, ask, bring about, have the sense they do. But the notion of the background itself can be applied at different levels. There is a background understanding underlying our everyday coping as bodily beings in our surroundings, which we have described in the previous chapters, and by which we make sense of our surroundings as figure and ground, zones of confinement and zones of openness, obstacles and facilitations. This kind of background is shared by human beings generally, and is articulated around the life meanings.

But we can also speak of the background understanding of a given culture, that is, the general understanding of what matters in human life, in the context of which things have the ethical, moral, and spiritual point that they do. For certain aboriginal societies, the extreme importance they attribute to certain places, their refusal to trade them for other (to us rootless and globalized economic agents) even more favorable places (so that, say, we can drill for oil under their original home), can only be understood if we can grasp the way in which their very identity is defined by this mountain, say, which in turn makes sense only because of their relation to the spirit world and its nature.

We take Gadamer's notion of horizon to be referring, anyway in this context, to a general understanding of this latter, cultural sort. But the concept has a complexity and a flexibility which are essential to it. On one hand, horizons can be identified and distinguished; it is through such distinctions that we can come to grasp what is distorting understanding and impeding communication. But on the other hand, horizons evolve, change. There is no such thing as a fixed horizon. "The horizon is, rather, something into which we move and which moves with us. Horizons change for a person who

7. Hans-Georg Gadamer, *Wahrheit und Methode* (Tübingen: Mohr, 1975), 289. *Truth and Method*, trans. Joel Weinsheimer, 2nd rev. ed. (New York: Continuum, 2004), 304.

is moving" (*Der Horizont ist vielmehr etwas, in das wir hineinwandern und das mit uns mitwandert. Dem Beweglichen verschieben sich die Horizonte*).[8] A horizon with unchanging contours is an abstraction. Horizons identified by the agents whose worlds they circumscribe are always in movement. The horizons of A and B may thus be distinct at time t, and their mutual understanding very imperfect. But A and B by living together may come to have a single common horizon at t + n.

In this way "horizon" functions somewhat like "language." We can talk about the "language of modern liberalism," or the "language of nationalism," and point out the things they cannot comprehend. But these are abstractions, freeze-frames of a continuing film. If we talk about the language of Americans or Frenchmen, we can no longer draw their limits a priori; for the language is identified by the agents, who can evolve.

We can see that this picture of horizons and their potential fusion yields a kind of "principle of charity": my interlocutor can't be totally wrong, nor can I, because we are inescapably in contact with reality, and can alter our "take" on it. But for all the surface similarities to Davidson's view, the arguments are really quite different. Gadamer's is ontologically based: human beings are in contact with the real. Davidson's is epistemological: the condition of my understanding you as you think and act in your terms is that I construe you as making sense in my terms most of the time. This has indeed the classical form of an antirealist thesis: in face of a commonsense distinction which seems to threaten us with irremediable ignorance about some important matter, take the bold step of denying the distinction.

The commonsense distinction in this case is that two societies or cultures may understand and make sense of their lives in very different ways. The disturbing possibility is that they may never be able to understand each other, may remain forever locked inside their own ways of sense-making. At its most disturbing, the prospect is that there is a human but alien culture which we can never grasp. What life is for them is ultimately unknowable to us. The antirealist response is to deny the distinction itself: there is no such thing as different, mutually irreducible ways of making sense of life, and therefore nothing which could even potentially play the role of unknowable object.

---

8. Gadamer, *Wahrheit und Methode*, 288. *Truth and Method*, 303.

We might think that the basis for charity doesn't count, that what matters is the conclusion. But in fact, the two principles have a fatefully different impact on the important issues of intercultural difference.

Davidson's argument against the idea that we could be imprisoned in utterly incongruent schemes is obviously a powerful one. Davidson's principle of charity requires that I, the observer/theorist, must make sense of him, the subject studied, in the sense of finding most of what he does, thinks, and says intelligible; else I can't be treating him as a rational agent, and there is nothing to understand, in the relevant sense, at all.

What this argument shows is that total unintelligibility of another culture is not an option. For to experience another group as unintelligible over some range of their practices, we have to find them quite understandable over other (very substantial) ranges. We have to be able to understand them as framing intentions, carrying out actions, trying to communicate orders, truths, etc. If we imagine even this away, then we no longer have the basis which allows us to recognize them as agents. But then there's nothing left to be puzzled about. Concerning non-agents, there is no question about what they're up to, and hence no possibility of being baffled on this score.

And clearly this kind of total noncomprehension is not possible for human beings. We can always count on instant communication around our nature as bodily agents, and the shared life needs, as we pointed out above. But the problem with Davidson's argument is that it is in a sense too powerful. It slays the terrifying mythical beast of total and irremediable incomprehensibility. But what we suffer from in our real encounters between peoples are the jackals and vultures of partial and (we hope) surmountable noncommunication.

In this real-life situation, Davidson's theory is less useful, mainly because it seems to discredit the idea of "conceptual schemes" altogether—this in spite of the fact that the argument only rules out our meeting a totally unintelligible one. But in dealing with the real, partial barriers to understanding, we need to be able to identify what is blocking us. And for this we need some way of picking out the systematic differences in construal between two different cultures, without either reifying these differences or branding them as ineradicable. This is because of two factors at play here: (1) what is blocking us is our failure to see the point of the human meanings they respond to, and (2) these meanings are interrelated in a gestalt holism; we can only understand particular points in relation to the broader sense of what is ultimately important.

This is what is taken into account in Gadamer's image of the horizon. Horizons can be different, but at the same time they can travel, change, extend—as you climb a mountain, for instance. It is what Davidson's position as yet lacks.

Without this, Davidson's principle of charity is vulnerable to being abused to ethnocentric ends. The principle tells me to make the best sense I can of the other's words and deeds. In translating his words into my language, I should render him so that as much as possible he speaks the truth, makes valid inferences, etc. But the issue is to know what counts as "my language" here. It can mean the language I speak at the moment of encounter. Or it can mean the extended language, the one that emerges from my attempts to understand him, to fuse horizons with him. If we take it in the first way, it is almost certain that I will ethnocentrically distort him.

For the problem is that the standing ethnocentric temptation is to make too quick sense of the stranger, that is, sense in one's own terms. The lesser breeds are without the law, because they have nothing we recognize as law. The step to branding them as lawless and outlaw is as easy as it is invalid and fateful. Thus when the Conquistadores met the Aztecs these hard-bitten, unscrupulous adventurers were deeply shaken by the Aztecs' practice of human sacrifice. For the more unsophisticated Spaniards, the only possible account of this was that the Aztecs worshipped the devil. "It's simple, *compadres*, you either worship God or the devil. Ripping out hearts, is that worshipping God?? It follows . . ."

The problem with Davidson's approach is that it allows us to forget, or to fail to appreciate from the beginning, how deeply we are failing to get the point of what they do. It allows us too easily to assume that the points of their actions are already available to us in our repertory of sense.

What is needed is not the Davidsonian "principle of charity"—which means: make the best sense of them in what we understand as sense—but rather: coming to understand that there is a very different way of understanding human life, the cosmos, the holy, etc. Somewhere along the line, you need some place in your ontology for something like "the Aztec way of seeing things," in contrast to "our way of seeing things"—in short, something like the scheme-content distinction. To fail to make this can be, literally, lethal.

Of course, this kind of ethnocentrism totally violates Davidson's intent. But the problem is that we need to understand how we move from our language at the time of encounter, which can only distort them, to a richer language which has place for them, from making the "best sense" in our initial terms, which will usually be an alien imposition, to making the best sense within a fused horizon. We can't see how we can conceive of or carry out this process without allowing into our ontology something like alternative horizons or conceptual schemes. This we think marks the superiority of Gadamer's view over Davidson's.

But Davidson's argument is nonetheless very valuable, in pointing out the dangers, even the paradoxes, involved in using any such terms. We can see this when we ask the question, what does the concept "scheme" contrast with? The term "content" is certainly very bad—as though there were stuff already lying there, to be framed in different schemes. There is certainly a deep problem here.

It belongs to the very idea of a scheme, in the sense one is tempted to use it in intercultural studies, that it indicate some systematic way in which people are interpreting or understanding their world. Different schemes are such incompatible ways of understanding the same things.

But what things? runs the objection. How can you point to the things in question? If you use the language of the target society to get at them, then all distinction between scheme and content disappears. But what else can you use? Well, let's say our language, that of us the observers/scientists, about this target area. But then we still won't have got at the "content" we share in common, which would have to be somehow identifiable independently of both schemes.

The point is well taken; and it needs to be kept in mind in order to avoid certain easy pitfalls, such as thinking that one has a neutral, universal categorization of the structures or functions of all societies ("political system," "family," "religion," etc.) which provides the ultimately correct description for what all the different fumbling, cultural languages are aiming at—as it were, the noumena to their phenomenal tongues. But the notion of two schemes, one target area, remains valid and, indeed, indispensable.

Let's go back to the case of the Conquistadores and the Aztecs. We might say that one thing the Conquistadores had right was that they recognized that all that ripping out of hearts in some way corresponded in Spanish society to the Church and the Mass, and that sort of thing. That is, the right insight, yielding a good starting point for an eventual fusion of horizons, involves identifying what something in the puzzling life of an alien people can usefully be contrasted with in ours. In Gadamerian terms, what we are doing is identifying that facet of our lives which their strange customs interpolate, challenge, offer a notional alternative to.

An example will show what is at stake here. A few years ago a wildly reductivistic American social scientist produced a theory of Aztec sacrifice in which it was explained "materialistically" in terms of their need for protein.[9] On this view the right point of comparison in Spanish society would be their slaughterhouses rather than their churches. Needless to say, from such a starting point, one gets nowhere.

The fruitful supposition is that what went on atop those pyramids reflected a very different construal of an X which overlaps with what Christian faith and practice is a construal of in Spain. This is where thinking, inquiry, can usefully start. It has one very powerful—and in principle challengeable—presupposition: that we share the same humanness, and that therefore we can ultimately find our feet in Aztec sacrifice, because it's a way of dealing with a human condition we share. Once this is accepted, then the notion of two schemes, same X, becomes inescapable. Only we have to be careful what we put in the place of the "X."

In a general proposition, we might say: dimension, or aspect of the human condition. In the particular case, it is much more dangerous to specify. "Religion" would be an obvious candidate word. But the danger is precisely that we happily take on board everything which this word means in our world, and slide back towards the ethnocentric reading of the Conquistadores. So we perhaps retreat to something vaguer, like "numinous." But even this carries its dangers.

The point is to beware of labels here. This is the lesson to be learned from attacks on the scheme-content distinction. But that the Mass and Aztec sacrifice belong to rival construals of a dimension of the human condition for which we have no stable, culture-transcendent name, is a thought we cannot let go of, unless we want to relegate these people to the kind of unintelligibility that members of a different species would have for us. If rejecting the distinction means sliding into this, it is hardly an innocent step.

9. Marvin Harris. *Cannibals and Kings: The Origins of Cultures.* (New York: Random House, 1977), 182.

2

We can see from this Gadamer-Davidson comparison that Gadamer has identified what we lack when we stare uncomprehending across a cultural gap. (1) We can't grasp the point of what they do, and (2) we will only be able to do this when we can understand the general shape of their sense of what things are ultimately or crucially important. But the word "scheme" can be misleading for this, not just in the way explored in the last section, but also because it seems to imply that this sense is formulated exclusively in concepts or propositions.

But this is crucially wrong. It seems to be the case that a people couldn't organize their lives around a given sense of the ultimately important without conceptual formulations; but it is very far from being the case that they exclusively do so. Rather this sense exists in what we called above a "multimedia" formulation. At one level, we have what Bourdieu calls "habitus," the way we can be trained to hold ourselves, stand in the presence of others, address them in a certain tone, and the like. For instance, we train our youth to stand respectfully before their elders, to bow at appropriate moments, not to raise their voices, to use certain forms of address. In all this, they learn to respect, even revere, their parents and elders. Or women are trained always to look at the ground in the company of men, never to look them straight in the face, etc., hence to assume a subordinate position, and not to challenge them.[10]

But learning this kind of habitus is not just a matter of learning certain movements. It is learning certain social meanings through such training. Thus the kids would not have learned if they didn't get the point that certain appropriate feelings and attitudes go along with this demeanor, that certain valuations are consonant with their way of acting and others not. Thus, if I, as a young person, am filled with contempt for my elders even as I conform, I recognize right off that this is something I must hide, that I am in fact dissimulating as I bow, that there is some conflict within me as I go on conforming to the norms—that I am an inner rebel.

Another way of seeing this point is that I don't conform just by making movements of a certain neutral description. The movements are meant to embody respect. That's why there are ways of carrying them through in such

---

10. Bourdieu, *Le Sens Pratique* (Paris: Minuit, 1980).

a perfunctory or even jaunty fashion that I am actually being cheeky, and hence violating the norm.

So the habitus here is a medium of expression of certain human meanings, defining a certain social world with its constitutive sense of what is important. It is also what integrates me into this social world, and makes those meanings manifest and real for me, as a child growing up. And there are other modes of expression/integration/manifestation. These include "theoretical" statements about older people, that they are worthy of respect, and why; they include: symbols and recognized symbolic connections, headdresses of elders, rituals they engage in, etc; and they also include: stories people tell, legends, cautionary tales, etc. All of these interpenetrate and mutually affect each other. The kind of respect I feel, as a well-brought-up boy, will be deeply colored by that story of an exemplary elder, and the love and admiration his children showed him, which deeply impressed me as a child; by some striking formulations of the idea that men grow wiser; by some saintly figure I met when I was a mere kid. We have here what we described in Chapter 2 as a multimedia grasp on meanings.

This interweaving of the bodily, the symbolic, and the narrative and propositional illustrates what we said above about the inseparability of the life and human meanings in the stream of human existence. The habitus itself, a bodily comportment which is the expression/manifestation of the most important social meanings, shows how the two levels are welded together. On one level, we can describe our maintaining equilibrium as our finding our footing in the gravitational field, which empowers us to act, move about, manipulate things. But from the very beginning of human life, this upright posture also becomes the site of human meanings, of understandings of dignity, for instance (as against the "humiliation" of being forced close to the ground), or of our relation to something higher, to heaven, say; and this can be developed and embroidered in different ways in a philosophy or a theology.[11]

11. This investment by human meanings of the body shows how it is possible *both* to say that there are universally recognizable human needs and actions, based on our common biological constitution, *and* that each culture transforms all our bodily gestures and actions in line with the human meanings it defines, as some philosophers, such as Merleau-Ponty and Foucault, have claimed. Even the most "basic" actions—how people eat, how they express sexual desire, how they enter into conversation with each other—partake of a

The body is, in particular, the site of social meanings, because of what we can call intercorporeality, the ways in which our bodies are attuned to each other from the very beginning of human life. A baby imitates the smile of her mother's face, well before she can grasp by observation her own face, and see the likeness of her expression to the mother's. In Merleau-Ponty's example, "a fifteen-month-old baby opens his mouth when I playfully take one of his fingers in my mouth and pretend to bite it. And yet, he has hardly even seen his face in a mirror and his teeth do not resemble mine. His own mouth and teeth such as he senses them from within are immediately for him the instruments for biting, and my jaw such as he sees it from the outside is for him immediately capable of the same intentions" (*un bébé de quinze mois ouvre la bouche si je prends par jeu l'un de ses doigts entre les dents et que je fasse mine de mordre. Et pourtant, il n'a guère regardé son visage dans une glace, ses dents ne ressemblent pas aux miennes. C'est que sa propre bouche et ses dents, telles qu'il les sent de l'intérieur, sont d'emblée pour lui des appareils à mordre, et que ma mâchoire, telle qu'il la voit du dehors, est d'emblée pour lui capable des mêmes intentions*).[12] The sense of possible intentions in one's own body and the perception of these in others are primordially understood as belonging to the same type, and the likeness is lived in the communion of a two-person game, before it is grasped as a classification. We are readied from the beginning to enter into dialogical rhythms and common actions with others, playing endlessly repetitive games of hiding and revealing, of concealment and surprise, and this prepares the ground for the future postures of intimacy and distance, of common action and separate projects, which shape the geography of later social life.

We mentioned in Chapter 5 that the different stances of disengagement were elaborated in language. We can extend that to the full range of human

---

different style in different cultures, and the outsider is always in danger of making the most egregious faux pas. Nevertheless we rarely have trouble recognizing the kind of action it is on this "basic" level, so much do the styles come across as variations on a common theme. We usually know that they're eating, or even looking hungrily at food—however different, for instance, are the styles of polite eating (quietly here, slurping and burping there), or the rules of commensality—or how eating relates to their human meanings (culture A has an important place for sacred meals, culture B not at all).

12. Merleau-Ponty, *Phénoménologie de la Perception*, 404. *Phenomenology of Perception*, 368.

meanings—moral, political, aesthetic, religious. But in saying this, we have to be taking language in a broad enough sense to include those bodily practices which reflect and embody these meanings, such as the bowing of our youth above. Language in this broad sense groups the ensemble of media which have constitutive force, that is, which can make meanings manifest for us. As we argued in Chapter 2, human meaning is in fact embedded in the whole gamut of media, in declarative speech, story, symbol, in rules, and in habitus.

And here we connect with the Gadamerian thesis that the world we live in, the human meanings we experience, are essentially constituted in language, in the broad sense of the previous paragraph. This is the Gadamerian thesis of "linguisticality" or *Sprachlichkeit.*

The broad sense of "language" we are forced to use here (or else we must use another term, but with this wide meaning) points up another problem with the term "conceptual scheme." The differences between human cultures can't be tracked simply at the level of the descriptive concepts which figure in their languages, in the narrow (ordinary) sense. This seems to be what Davidson is assuming in his discussion that we cited above.[13] "Incommensurable schemes" would have to mean "not intertranslatable" languages.[14] But if we think of two speakers who face a world whose features are equally accessible to both, in virtue of similar capacities of perception, identification, etc., it is hard to imagine a serious case of real non-intertranslatability. Suppose my interlocutor does classify things differently; suppose he says, "Look at that handsome yawl," as the boat sails by, where he should have said "ketch" using standard English. If his line of sight is good, and it is likely that he "has made no mistake at all about the position of the jigger on the passing yacht," I just assume that he suffers from a form of malapropism, and that "ketch" in ordinary parlance has become "yawl" in his lexicon.[15] Translation has been achieved.

But once we take account of the discussion in Chapter 5, and see how rather different genres of discourse and language games come to develop in the course of human history, once we see that these language games invoke

13. Davidson, "On the Very Idea."
14. Ibid., 190.
15. Ibid., 196.

meanings which are expressed and manifested in a broader range of media than just descriptive prose, we can see how fragile the assumption is that speakers face a world whose features are equally accessible to all. This may be true of what J. L. Austin called "medium-sized dry goods," but what about the Persian visitor, who thought he was competent in Greek, who hears Socrates interrogating Thrasymachus (or the unsophisticated visitor from Magara, for that matter)? What about the Spaniards discovering Aztec sacrifice? They can be given a word: "this is dialectic," or "this is N (whatever the Nahuatl word is for this activity)." But this doesn't help, certainly doesn't help enough, because there is still something baffling about what this is supposed to describe—the activity itself, or the descriptions of things (like "aporia," or "proper sacrificial victim") which figure in the activity.

But, it might be objected, we can't expect these strangers to know everything. Just being baffled can't be a sufficient condition for non-intertranslatability. We are often out of our depth when we enter special milieu even in our own culture. In a chemical laboratory, or a cyclotron, I would be totally out of it, unable to understand what people were saying. We don't see a cultural gap here, because I presumably understand in general terms what post-Galilean science is all about,; how it yields a deeper grasp on the processes which go on in medium-sized dry goods. I know how to place this exchange, even if I lack the specialized knowledge to follow it. (But we do sometimes speak with C. P. Snow of "two cultures" here,[16] when we want to emphasize broad differences in outlook and value between people trained in science and the humanities.)

In other words, we—unlike a medieval peasant suddenly entering our century through some time warp—understand what the point of this activity is. But that is just what escapes the Persian and the Spaniard in our examples. This difference is certainly reflected in descriptive terms which are non-intertranslatable, like "dialectic" and "aporia," or (the Nahuatl terms we roughly translate as) "sacrifice" and "victim." But the differences are linguistic at a deeper level. The activities themselves are constituted in language, in certain forms of discourse or exchange, before, or perhaps simultaneously with, their description. We could imagine that when Socrates started his

16. C. P. Snow, *The Two Cultures and the Scientific Revolution* (New York: Cambridge University Press, 1959).

(irritating and challenging) mode of questioning, the term "dialectic" had not yet been coined. Perhaps in fact it was Plato who coined it later. The Aztec sacrifice that shocked Cortés and his men evolved out of ritual languages, rich interweavings of gesture, symbol, and verbal exchange, which had come to express/constitute certain meanings in human-divine relations.

Learning another language can't just be coming to master a descriptive lexicon for the things which lie before us, equally accessible to all human beings. There are such things—rabbits, elephants, trees, hands, feet, edible fruit—and they tremendously help communication on first encounter. But that's not all there is to mutual understanding. Deep incommensurability, or non-intertranslatability,[17] comes when we can't make sense of big segments of their discourse, or of some of their crucial language games. To go beyond this, we need to grasp something which goes way beyond what we could ever puzzle out by comparing their descriptive vocabulary to the world-as-it-is-accessible-to-us; we have to grasp how in the whole range of media they constitute human meanings, some of which are initially very foreign to us.

Thus some of their words may be very hard to construe, because they don't just belong to but crucially help constitute certain of their central practices. Take an example which has been very important to us politically: the type of régime which has come down to us from the Greek polis (and to some extent also the Roman Republic), where there is a fundamental equality between the citizens qua citizens, equality which is essential to their conception of free self-rule and a free people. This type of régime is impossible without there being some formulation of the demand for equality, without this becoming a term of assessment, held to apply to certain societies, or certain contexts, and not others. We could imagine certain kinds of primitive society where what we could call equality could exist unformulated, but not

---

17. Of course, that a term in L can't be translated into L' is something which holds only for L' at a certain time (where L' is a natural language). This is so because languages can neologize and can be extended and developed, as we saw. It is significant that some of the concepts from cultures rather far from ours enter our language through our domesticating the word, along with ethnographic explanations. Words like *mana*, *tabu*, and *seppuku* illustrate this. Of course, just taking over their word may not help, as we see with the case of *tabu*, which we bandy around freely in a way which has little relation to the original Polynesian. See Marshall Sahlins, *Social Stratification in Polynesia* (Seattle: University of Washington Press, 1958).

for example a Greek polis, where equality was bound up with the norms for who should rule and how, and where it thus had to be recognized in some form as a norm.

Thus the Spartans describing themselves as the Equals (*homoioi*), the norm of *isêgoria* in democracies, the battle around *isonomia*, and the like are not accessory features which we could imagine having been quite absent while those societies remained essentially what they were. The self-description as equals is an essential part of this régime, that is, of this relation of equality, and this because the régime requires a degree of explicit common understanding which is impossible without self-description.

This is an example of what we could call the constitutive dimension of language. There are ways in which the language we use enters into, is an essential part of, our feelings, our goals, our social relations and practices. The aspect of language which is essential in this way may be purely an expressive aspect in some cases, such as when modes of address carry the burden of marking the kinds of footing we are on with each other. But it may also be that what is essential to a given feeling or relation is certain descriptions.

This is what we see in the case of the polis. Self-description as equals is essential to the régime. And this not in virtue of some merely causal condition, as one might say that relative isolation or an infrastructure of slave labor were essential to these régimes. Rather the point is that this kind of practice of equality essentially requires the explicit recognition of equality. It would not be classifiable as this practice without that recognition, without the participants holding each other to it as a norm.

Put another way, the norm can't be understood independently of a certain set of practices, here of citizen self-rule; and the practices are unthinkable without the norm. Without grasping this constitutive relation, the outside observer has no adequate sense of the descriptive meaning.

Visitors from some totally despotic culture, dropped into classical Athens, we keep hearing people using this word "equal," and its companion "like" (*isos, homoios*). We know how to apply these words to sticks, stones, perhaps also houses and ships; for there is a tolerably exact translation in our home language (let's say Persian again). And we also know some ways of applying them to human beings, for instance physical likeness or equality of height. But there is a peculiar way these Hellenes have of using the words which baffles us. Indeed, they have a pugnacious and perverse way of applying them to human beings who seem to us not at all alike, some tall and some short, some of noble birth, some base, and so on.

What we have to grasp is how these words get their grip in politics. Maybe it is not hard for us to see that these short, base men are refusing to knuckle under to the taller nobility. That much will be evident from the aggressive gestures, and perhaps the actual fighting which goes on. But what we cannot yet grasp is the perceived positive value of this mode of life. Indeed, this conflict can appear to us as just strife, a sign of impending breakdown; we cannot see a different and viable mode of life here at all. (Similarly, some early eighteenth-century Frenchmen thought that England must be on the verge of breakdown, once it allowed the insanely contradictory institution of "His Majesty's Loyal Opposition.")

We have to grasp the ideal of a people of free agents, that is, one in which none of the full participants just takes orders from someone, which agents must therefore rule themselves, and yet which have the courage, initiative, and patriotism to get it together when they have to fight for their freedom. These agents exercise their right to deliberate together about what they will do, but the right to talk does not make them any less effective as agents and warriors when it comes to act.[18] We do not yet see, in other words, the nobility of this kind of life, or what its practitioners identify as noble, their conception of the dignity of a man (here they very much meant men, free adult males) residing in his being this kind of agent, having this kind of freedom.

A similar point could be made in connection with certain of their uses of the word "freedom." Let us take another observer, hostile to the polis, writing many centuries later in defense of a despotic order. The notion of freedom, as a status within a certain kind of practice of self-rule, seemed to him utterly devoid of sense. Freedom could only mean the absence of physical obstacles, and this might be extended to include the absence of legal prohibitions.[19]

What our Persian observer could not see, and what Hobbes would not see, is the way in which "equal," "like," "free," and such terms as "citizen" help define a horizon of value. They articulate the citizens' sensitivity to the

---

18. Cf. Pericles' funeral oration in Thucydides, *Peloponnesian War*, Book II, 34–6.
19. Thomas Hobbes, *Leviathan* (Oxford: Oxford University Press, 2008), chap. 21.

standards intrinsic to this ideal and way of life. These articulations are constitutive of this way of life, and therefore we cannot understand it unless we understand these terms.

But reciprocally, we cannot understand these terms unless we grasp what kind of sensitivity they are articulating. They cannot be understood simply on the representational model, as potential descriptions of an independent reality—predicates which can be "satisfied" or not by certain independently existing objects. They function, true, to describe certain social conditions and relations. But these conditions and relations only exist because the agents involved recognize certain concerns, defined in a certain way; they could not sustain just these relations and states if they did not. But the terms are themselves essential to these concerns, under this definition, being recognized. It is through them that the horizon of concern of the agents in question is articulated in the way it must be for just these practices, conditions, relations to exist.

Hence to understand what these terms represent, to grasp them in their representative function, we have to understand them in their articulating-constitutive function. We have to see how they can bring a certain horizon of concern to a certain articulation.

How do we manage to do this? There is no formula; but one thing that should be evident is that one cannot make any headway unless one engages with the people concerned. In order to penetrate their discourse, one has to start trying to hold discourse with them. These exchanges will be rather primitive at first, centered on the equally accessible things; but only through them can we approach exchanges which will get closer to those in which their human meanings are constituted. That is what is deeply mistaken in the way that Quine and Davidson pose the problem of language learning. "Radical translation" (Quine) or "radical interpretation" (Davidson) supposes a learning situation in which the learner observes what the speaker says, as well as its context, and what precedes and follows it. The stance is the same as that of the practitioner of science: observer to object. We could just see this working, if the task were to calibrate their vocabulary for medium-sized dry goods with our own, but never if we're trying to understand what ends and meanings give point to their lives and practices. The insistence that "our actual scheme and language are best understood as extensional and materialist"[20] also makes sense on this restrictive assumption about our goal,

20. Davidson, "On the Very Idea," 188.

but it is hard to see even what it could mean if our aim is to understand what they're about.

This is where Gadamer's approach is greatly superior. Gadamer makes central the paradigm of a "conversation," in his understanding of human science, rather than that of an inquiring subject studying an object. Success comes, not with an adequate theory of the object, but with the "fusion of horizons," as we said above. This view fully takes account of the point made in the previous paragraph, that we can only bridge certain gaps in understanding by engaging with the relevant others. Moreover, this exchange has to be on some more or less level footing, or it risks serious distortion. And third, in the process of understanding, both sides can well find their previous self-understandings challenged and upset.

This last result will often arise, because in coming to understand activities with a point which is initially strange and incomprehensible, we will often upset our implicit notions of what is "normal" or humanly possible. The cultural pictures which held us captive about the range of human possibility will have to go if we are to accommodate this new way of being without distorting it. We come to see that just understanding this sacrifice as worshipping the Devil is blocking us, and at once this catchall account of strange religions has to be abandoned. Our typology is blown wide open.

In general we might say that in order to get over the distortion, we have to see that there were other possibilities, that our way of being isn't the only or "natural" one, but that it represents one among other possible forms. We can no longer relate to our way of doing or construing things "naïvely," as just too obvious to mention.

If understanding the other is to be construed as fusion of horizons and not as possessing a science of the object, then the slogan might be: no understanding the other without a changed understanding of self.

The kind of understanding that ruling groups have of the ruled, that conquerors have of the conquered—most notably in recent centuries in the far-flung European empires—has usually been based on a quiet confidence that the terms they need are already in their vocabulary. Much of the "social science" of the last century is in this sense just another avatar of an ancient human failing. And indeed, the satisfactions of ruling, beyond the booty, the unequal exchange, the exploitation of labor, very much includes the reaffirmation of one's identity which comes from being able to live this fiction without meeting brutal refutation. Real understanding always has an identity cost—something the ruled have often painfully experienced. It is a feature of tomorrow's world (we hope) that this cost will now be less un-equally distributed.

The cost appears as such from the standpoint of the antecedent identity, of course. It may be judged a gain once one has gone through the change. We are also enriched by knowing what other human possibilities there are in our world. It cannot be denied, however, that the path to acknowledging this is frequently painful.

The crucial moment is the one where we allow ourselves to be interpolated by the other—where the difference escapes from its categorization as an error, a fault, or a lesser, undeveloped version of what we are, and challenges us to see it as a viable human alternative. It is this which unavoidably calls our own self-understanding into question. This is the stance Gadamer calls "openness," as against the way I stand to what I see as an object of science, where I try "reflecting [myself] out of [my] relation to the other and so becoming unreachable by him" (*sich selber aus der Beziehung zum anderen herauszureflektieren und dadurch von ihm unerreichbar zu warden*),[21] "Openness to the other ... involves recognizing that I myself must accept some things that are against me, even though no one else forces me to do so" (*Offenheit für den anderen schliesst ... die Anerkennung ein, dass ich in mir etwas gegen mich gelten lassen muss, auch wenn es keinen anderen gäbe, der es gegen mich geltend machte*).[22]

Gadamer in challenging the subject-object model of human science with his "conversation" paradigm has shown the crucial importance of equal exchange if there is to be a real surmounting of cultural barriers.[23]

3

In addition, the confidence, one might say faith, in our capacity to communicate with each other, even across great differences of culture, arises on the basis of Gadamer's fundamental thesis of linguisticality (*Sprachlichkeit*). We

---

21. Gadamer, *Wahrheit und Methode*, 342. *Truth and Method*, 354.

22. Gadamer, *Wahrheit und Methode*, 343. *Truth and Method*, 355.

23. For further discussion, see Charles Taylor, "Understanding the Other: A Gadamerian View on Conceptual Schemes," in *Dilemmas And Connections: Selected Essays*. (Cambridge, MA: Belknap Press of Harvard University Press, 2011), chapter 2.

were only inducted into our home culture through learning a language, in the broad sense adumbrated above. But as human beings we are also capable of learning other languages. So however different and even mutually repugnant are the meanings of our respective worlds, we can always in principle come to understand the other. We say "in principle," because it is obvious that in practice this may be extremely difficult, and that conflict, fear, unequal power, arrogance, and a host of other such obstacles may prevent us doing so here and now.

What underlies the possibility of learning other languages, if indeed we do possess it? For we have to bear in mind that nothing guarantees that we would be able to see the point of just any way of life. We can imagine alien beings whose moral/spiritual meanings, if indeed we can even use these terms, would be quite opaque to us. And in partial ways, we can see something like this inability to understand even between humans. We might be vigorously discussing the beauty of Mozart's late piano concerti, or the spiritual depth of Beethoven's late quartets, and a totally tone-deaf person will be unable to understand or take part in the conversation. We may imagine that the difficulty is insurmountable in this case. But something of the same blank incomprehension might be felt by a neophyte to Western music, even though he or she might be able to fuse horizons with us later.

That we are able to bridge vast gulfs of cultural difference, even though it may require much effort and time, is a remarkable fact that we perhaps don't sufficiently examine and wonder at. Our situation seems to be this: all normal human babies are born with this potential, to be integrated into one or other cultural understanding of human meanings through being inducted into a language and way of life ("language" in the broad sense above). The potential can only be realized through such an induction, hence must be realized in one particular variant. But (1) we know that this child could have been inducted with success in any other culture, if he or she had been brought up there, and (2) he or she can learn a second culture.

This means that, however strongly marked by the expressing/integrating/manifesting forms of one culture, human beings are not imprisoned in them. They are not imprisoned in them, because they retain something of the original capacity to understand and be inducted into any of them. There is here another kind of contact, analogous to the one we have been pointing to in our everyday coping with our world. Just as Johnny, for instance, is not imprisoned in any particular set of beliefs about his surroundings, because he has this basic capacity, through his primordial commerce with things, to go and check what he has been told, so Sarah is not imprisoned in individualist Western culture, but can go as an anthropologist to the outback and come to understand what it means to have an identity defined by totem animals and sacred geography. The contact here consists in an original and as yet uncanceled human capacity to resonate with certain meanings, those within the human range—a range which could only be defined by seeing into what artificially designed cultural forms human babies could or could not be inducted. (Needless to say, no one will ever make the necessary experiments; and if they proposed to do so, they should be put in jail.)

The "contact" in one case consists of actual dealings with the world, and enables us to get behind our representations (formulated beliefs); in the other case, it consists of a capacity to respond, resonate with, make sense of human meanings; and it enables us to get beyond and beneath, not so much representations—though they are involved here—but a kind of imprinting, whereby a certain range of meanings have become for us the human meanings. And these two abilities are intertwined at their root in our most basic bodily comportments.

We can speculate what underlies this capacity to grasp the human meanings, and a wide range of accounts is available. Some of these focus on an intrinsic human nature, perhaps conceived in evolutionary terms, or else connected to our rational capacities. Others have recourse to something outside ourselves. Starting perhaps from the sense of being related to something beyond and above, a sense which can inhere in our upright posture, they conceive this higher reality in very different ways: as the God invoked in the Jewish-Christian-Muslim tradition, or as Nirvana and the unreality of the self; or the great current of life running through the cosmos, evoked by Wordsworth in one way, and Dostoyevsky in another; and so on through a host of other hypotheses. We will almost certainly find it impossible to settle finally on any one of these; and maybe all are wrong. But the phenomenon they are trying to explain is real and important, and we have a distorted view of the intercultural dialogue if we lose sight of it.

Gadamer writes in the wake of Heidegger's pathbreaking work. His "principle of charity" is informed by a contact theory. Our different worlds are linguistically constituted, but our languages are responding to something, trying to articulate something in the human condition. If we want to say that language or culture, in forming our worlds, mediates our contact with the universe and with our human nature, we would have to add that our language doesn't exhaust this contact. Rather it arises first, against the background or context of our animal existence, following the urgings of instinct in coming to grips with our surroundings; and second, it comes as a specification of a more general capacity, which can never be totally lost, to be inducted into one or other particular variant of the human meanings.

That is why we are never imprisoned in a single language, why we can find our feet in others, can ultimately make sense of what they are talking about, of the meanings they disclose, even if after much time and effort. We are not imprisoned, because language- and world making are not arbitrary; they are in response to something. This is the point of the Heideggerian image that humans are "the shepherds of Being."[24] And in each case the something in question is not irremediably hidden from other human beings, however puzzling, difficult, and repugnant it seems. At least, this last claim is the object of a kind of humanist faith.

Of course, mutual understanding in this sense doesn't yet amount to a "fusion of horizons" in Gadamer's sense. I can learn a foreign language, or learn to find my feet in another culture, without being able to translate from that language, or explain that culture to my compatriots. Being bilingual or bicultural is one thing, but being able to calibrate one of our languages or cultures on the other is quite another. To say that languages are incommensurable is to say that many things said in one can't be translated into the other. Just the fact that I have learned both doesn't stop them being so.

What Gadamer understood as a "fusion" is a further stage, where we come to be able to situate one set of human meanings in relation to the other, where we can even elaborate a common set of terms in which the different fundamental options of each can be related to the other. In the process, we extend our original home languages, enrich their vocabulary, enlarge their gamut of reference points, so that they become capable of carrying this wider understanding. Anthropology and historiography are full of such attempts at languages of perspicuous contrast, such as the distinction between "shame" and "guilt" cultures, or between gift exchange à la Marcel Mauss and economic exchange.

24. Martin Heidegger, *The Question Concerning Technology, and Other Essays*, trans. William Lovitt (New York: Harper & Row, 1977), 42.

But as these examples indicate, these attempts are always fragile and sub-ject to challenge. We are never completely sure that we haven't distorted one or other of the cultures compared. And it is certainly highly possible that some of these differences will forever resist calibration. Indeed, it is an es-sential part of the position we adopt, "plural realism," which we shall explain further in Chapter 8, that the possibility of ultimate noncalibration must be kept open. Only time and unremitting effort can tell us what can or cannot be achieved in this area. There are no a priori assurances either way.

But prior to, and as a condition of, any attempted fusion, comes the kind of understanding of the initially strange other, which is grounded in our common ability, as human, linguistic animals, to learn. A "principle of char-ity" does emerge from this condition, properly understood. It is grounded in a contact theory, and reposes finally on an unproblematic "realism." It can allow for the striking gaps and incommensurabilities which actually show up between human cultures, while making it understandable that we can in fact often come to straddle them, even if we can't go beyond this to fuse them.

The difficulties of Davidson's principle, on the other hand, come from his continued embedding in the mediational picture, so that his proof that there cannot be inaccessible conceptual schemes takes the form of a standard antirealist argument: the conditions of the possibility of our understanding of others' meanings as meanings rules out our even recognizing a radically other conceptual scheme. One has to break the captivity within this me-diational picture in order to come to grips in a fruitful way with the issues of intercultural understanding. This is one among many examples of how important it is to identify and escape from this mediational *Bild*, which has become so powerfully entrenched in modern culture.

CHAPTER SEVEN

Realism Retrieved

SO FAR we have argued that, once freed from the mediational picture, we can see that we are in unmediated touch with everyday reality. We can now add that, since the mediational view provides the context in which the whole complex of issues around "realism" and "antirealism" make sense, they lose this sense if you escape from this construal. Or perhaps better put, one awakes to an unproblematic realism with respect to the world, no longer a daring philosophical "thesis."

Paradoxically, however, once we further observe that the world is a co-production, that the objects we directly encounter are shaped by our bodily embedding in the everyday world, it looks like we can no longer make sense of the possibility of understanding things as they are in themselves independent of any interaction with human beings. Indeed, insofar as our everyday coping practices give us direct access to the *everyday world*, they seem to block all access to the *universe as it is in itself.*

Rorty is happy to embrace this new inner-outer distinction. He holds that we are, of course, confined to what can be encountered on the basis of our coping practices. We therefore can't think of science as a way of discovering an independent reality, and, luckily, we don't need to. Embedded coping is the only realism we can make sense of, and all the realism we need to make sense of science.

We, however, want to argue *both* for our embodied direct access to the things of the everyday world as they appear *to us* and a realist view of science as describing the things in the universe as they are *in themselves*, independent of their relation to our bodily capacities and our coping practices. Rorty focuses his opposition to our view in his challenge to Charles Taylor:

> Realism becomes interesting only when we supplement plain speech and common sense with the "in itself" versus "to us" distinction. Taylor sees me as bearing the burden of argument because he thinks that this latter distinction cannot simply be walked away from but must be dealt with. I think neither he nor anyone else has explained why we cannot just walk away from it. Such an explanation would have to tell us more than we have ever before been told about what good the distinction is supposed to do us. I keep hoping that Taylor, as fervent an anti-Cartesian as I, will join me in abandoning it. Alas, he persists in agreeing with Bernard Williams . . . and other admirers of Descartes that it is indispensable.[1]

Here we have the parting of the ways between a view like Rorty's, which we shall call *deflationary realism*, that claims that all objects, even those studied by natural science, are only intelligible on the background of our embedded coping, so that the idea of a view from nowhere is literally unintelligible, and our view, let us call it *robust realism*, that claims that, to understand the status of the structures studied by natural science, we have to make sense of an independent reality. From the perspective of the robust realist, deflationary realism is a kind of antirealism, which is a prisoner of a new inner-outer picture. It is no accident that Hilary Putnam once defended this form of realism as *internal* realism[2] (a view he has since abandoned).

But haven't we succumbed to the same logic? Isn't internal realism the only realism open to those who claim that we have direct access to the *everyday world* precisely because it is organized by and for embodied beings like ourselves? How can we claim that the primordial and unavoidable

1. Richard Rorty, "Charles Taylor on Truth," *Truth and Progress*, vol. 3 of *Philosophical Papers* (Cambridge: Cambridge University Press, 1998), 94.

2. Hilary Putnam, *Reason, Truth and History* (Cambridge: Cambridge University Press, 1981).

significances of things depend on our bodily existence in the world and, nonetheless, make sense of a science that claims to describe the components of the universe as they are in themselves, absolutely independent of any relation to our embodiment? If engaged experience is primordial and the disengaged mode is *derivative* from the engaged one, how can we hope to achieve or even approach a view from nowhere? It seems to follow, rather, that whatever we can encounter is a function of the kinds of bodies and needs we ineluctably have. How, then, can our unproblematic realism be anything but deflationary?

To answer these hard questions, we will have to accept Rorty's challenge that we tell "more than we have ever before been told about what good the ["in itself" versus "to us"] distinction is supposed to do us."[3] Standing on the shoulders of Merleau-Ponty and Samuel Todes, we will attempt to do just that.

We begin with the claim that the world of the agent is shaped by his or her bodily existence. But what does it mean to have your "world shaped" by something? This is a relation subtly different from the ordinary causal link with which it is sometimes confused. Let's focus on the way our world is shaped by our being bodily agents of the kind that we are. This is something different from the way some of our functions as agents are determined by physical causes. For instance, as a perceiving agent, I cannot now see the wall behind me. This can be explained by certain causal relations. The behavior of light and my physical constitution are so disposed as to make it impossible for the light reflected off the surface of the wall behind me to reach my retina. In this sense, my embodiment undoubtedly shapes my perception, and hence in a sense my "world."[4]

---

3. Rorty, "Charles Taylor on Truth," 94.

4. Not that there is a law-like correlation between light and sight. The electromagnetic radiation striking my retina is a necessary but not sufficient condition of my seeing the wall. To think otherwise is to commit what Merleau-Ponty calls the stimulus error of the empiricists. In the case of seeing the wall behind me, he points out that, although the retinal stimulation has sharp boundaries, my visual field has none, and that, as a matter of fact, we do sense the wall behind us, just as something we take to be a façade looks different from what we take to be a house. If I believed that there was a chasm behind me, the world in front of me would look different. See Merleau-Ponty, *Phenomenology of Perception,* trans. Donald A. Landes (Abingdon, Oxon: Routledge, 2012), 69–73.

But this is a rather different relation from the following example. As I sit here and take in the scene before me, it is oriented vertically: some things are "up," others are "down"; it is oriented also with respect to depth: some things are "near," others "far." Some objects "lie to hand," others are "out of reach"; some constitute "insurmountable obstacles" to movement, others are "easily displaced." My present position doesn't give me a "good purchase" on the scene; for that I would have to shift farther to the left. And so on.

Here is a world "shaped" by embodiment, in the sense that my way of experiencing or "living" the world is essentially that of an agent with our kind of body—an agent who seeks to remain upright, who can deal with things close up immediately, but only if they are in front of her; an agent who has to move to get to things farther away; who can grasp certain kinds of things easily and not others, can remove certain obstacles and not others, can move to make a scene more perspicuous, and so on. To say that our world is essentially that of our kind of agent is to say that the terms in which we describe our experience—for instance, those in quote marks in the previous paragraph—make sense only against the background of our kind of embodiment. To understand what it is to "lie to hand" you have to understand what it is to be an agent with the particular bodily capacities that humans have. Some creature from another planet might be unable to grasp this as a projectible term. Of course, it might work out some description which was roughly extensionally equivalent, but to project this term the way we do you have to understand what it is to be an embodied human being. Among other things, you have to have hands.

Thus, two quite different kinds of relationship might be expressed by saying that our experience is shaped by our bodily constitution. In the first—the case of the wall behind me—we note some consequences of this constitution for our experience however characterized. In the second, we point out how the nature of this experience is formed by this constitution, that is, how the terms in which this experience is described are given their sense only in relation to this form of embodiment. The first kind of relation is asserted in an ordinary statement of contingent causality. The second concerns by contrast the conditions of intelligibility of certain terms. It is this second relation that we want to invoke in speaking of our world being shaped by our body, culture, and form of life.

The impossibility of walking away from talk of things in themselves and truth as correspondence depends on discovering a third relation to the world besides causality and intelligibility. If one privileges causality one ends in naturalism. If one privileges intelligibility, either one claims that the objects of science are constituted by and derived from experience, as Husserl and Merleau-Ponty tend to do, and then phenomenology leads to idealism, or one claims, as Rorty does, that the objects of science are no more and no less independent of us than everyday things such as stepping stones, warm rooms, and sunsets, and one is imprisoned in deflationary realism.[5]

Making sense of science in a way compatible with the robust realism of most of its practitioners, requires understanding our embodiment in a way that allows us to make sense of the radically different ways we are engaged with the things in the everyday world and with the structures of the physical universe. Only then can we see how our understanding of things in themselves and truth as correspondence arises out of, but transcends, *both* our direct casual contact with the universe *and* our basic intelligible contact with the everyday world.

Consider what is involved in grasping and drinking from a glass that lies to hand. To begin with, I have to see the glass. This is no small feat. To perceive at all, we have to align ourselves with the causal powers of the physical universe. As embodied beings, we have to face what we are looking for, move to an appropriate distance given the size of the object, and assure an unencumbered line of sight to it. In this way, our skill spontaneously takes account of the fact that, as the causal theory of perception makes clear, in order to see an object, we have to be in a position to be causally acted on by light from it.

Thus, the universe constrains us to get in sync with it, and rewards us with sight only insofar as we conform to its demands. But we are so skilled at getting an optimal take on things that we normally overlook the fact that we once had to learn to align ourselves with the constraints of nature in order to perceive. Only if some disturbance leads us to recalibrate or move to a new position, can we notice that our activity of seeking a maximal perceptual grip bridges the gap between the causal influence of meaningless nature and our meaningful perceptual experience.

---

5. For an independently developed account of deflationary realism, see Arthur Fine's description of what he calls the natural ontological attitude. Fine, *The Shaky Game* (Chicago: University of Chicago Press, 1986).

To grasp the glass once we have a visual grip on it, we are obliged to conform our hand to its physical shape. And finally, to pick it up and raise it to our lips, our body must be set to take correct account of the weight of the glass. As John Searle points out, if we pick up a plastic beer mug thinking it is made of heavy pewter, we will end up throwing the beer over our shoulder. Indeed, all our activity and the whole top-bottom orientation of the everyday world must take gravity into account.

In general, Todes points out, we can perceive and act effectively only if we are correctly oriented in the earth's vertical field.

> Being oriented in respect to the vertical field itself, we can be properly or improperly so oriented. That is, we can be right side up or upside down in it. The vertical field is the field *in* which our body direction is oriented. On the other hand, being oriented in respect to objects in our horizontal field but not to the horizontal field itself, it makes no sense to speak of a generally proper or improper horizontal orientation. That is, it makes no sense to speak of our being left-side-right or front-side-back.[6]

> There is then a phenomenological priority of the world-field—in which we must orient our off-centered selves—over the horizontal field of our self-centered experience in the world. This priority is reflected by the phenomenological priority . . . of our capacity for proper vertical orientation, in the world, over our capacity for effective orientation toward objects in our horizontal field of experience in the world. Our capacity to stand up normally gives us the capacity to act; but not vice versa.[7]

Our relation to the influence of the vertical field turns out to be the most illuminating instance of the special combination of spontaneity and receptivity required in our stance to the universe in order for us to act effectively in the world.

> Our initial problem is neither to conform (accede) *to* this influence, nor to offer resistance *to* it—neither of which makes perceptual sense. Our problem is to orient ourselves effectively rather than ineffectively *in* this field of influence; to align ourselves in this field in such a way that it dependably enables us

6. Todes, *Body and World*, 123.
7. Ibid., 124.

to do what we need to do in it. . . . Balancing ourselves we *are held* vertically upright by the way we *hold ourselves* upright in relation to the steady vertical field of influence in which we stand. Balance is neither purely active, like moving, nor purely passive, like being moved. It is both active and passive, and one only through the other.[8]

The phenomenon of balance shows us that the determination of objects depends on us, but that we can effect this determination only insofar as we align ourselves with a truly independent reality.

But one can only see this if one uses phenomenology to get beneath the determinate and conceptually permeated perceptual world where analysis normally starts. Only by thus telling more than we have been told before in the history of philosophy, are we able to see what philosophers close to common sense like Aristotle have supposed all along, namely that we are in touch with the cosmos. But we now can see that it is not by having a disembodied, detached, contemplative capacity that we are thus in touch, but rather, thanks to an involved, active, material body that can orient itself appropriately to cope with things.

But the undaunted defender of deflationary realism will no doubt reply that, of course, we must be realists about the everyday world and the universe, but metaphysical talk of our beliefs corresponding to things as they are in themselves is, for that very reason, otiose. As Rorty puts it, "Taylor thinks that once one gets out from under epistemology one comes to an 'uncompromising realism.' I think one comes to a position in which the only version of 'realism' one has left is the trivial, uninteresting, and commonsensical one which says that all true beliefs are true because things are as they are."[9]

So, according to Rorty, there is nothing more we can say about what makes the propositions of science true than we can say about what makes our beliefs about everyday objects true. Both correspond to how things are, and to do so both depend on our embedding. It adds nothing to hold that truths about baseballs depend on our bodies and our cultural agreements,

8. Ibid., 125. Piotr Hoffman's introduction to *Body and World* highlights the importance of Todes's phenomenological account of balance as a way of saving phenomenology from the threat of idealism. We are greatly indebted to Todes's pathbreaking and convincing insight and Hoffman's appreciation of its importance.

9. Rorty, "Charles Taylor on Truth," 93–94.

while the truths of science describe things as they are totally independent of us and our everyday way of making sense of things.

If we were to take our beliefs as given and warranted only by other beliefs and didn't investigate how these beliefs were formed, Rorty would be right that a correspondence theory of truth adds nothing to what we already say when we affirm the truths of everyday assertions and of scientific theory. But this doesn't mean that talk of correspondence doesn't say anything important. It adds nothing, because it is an implicit part of the background understanding that underlies our pursuit of everyday knowledge and of science.

If we return to our most basic, primordial way of being in the world, where we are led to respond to the things in it as affordances, we understand ourselves as at grips with a world that aids us and at the same time sets limits on what we can do. We have to adopt the right stance to it; else we will suffer frustration or worse. The things that are showing up for us as obstacles, supports, facilitators, in short as affordances, have as it were an ontic solidity and depth. They set boundary conditions on our activities. They have what philosophy has come to call their "nature," which we have to respect and adjust ourselves to.

And that means that as well as showing up as affordances, things also bear other features; they have a structure that underlies what they afford us. To satisfy our needs, some things must be rigid, such as a club, or a stick to knock down fruit; others must be pliable, such as a comfortable bed of leaves. But the rigid things can weaken, and the pliable become hard and unyielding. What makes each kind of thing "normally" one or the other? And what makes them now one, now the other? To seek the answers to these questions is to explore the as-yet-hidden faces of these objects, which underlie or explain the face they turn to us.

Thus, our background understanding not only takes for granted that we are in contact with boundary conditions independent of us and our mode of making things intelligible; it also takes for granted that there is more to the objects of everyday experience than we will ever be able to make explicit, and that our experience of getting a grip on these everyday objects both reveals and conceals the structure that underlies and explains our experience of having to come to terms with something independent of us.

Still, Rorty and all deflationary realists can persist. If all we can say about the realism of our scientific truth claims is they are based on a background realism in our everyday experience, such truths will be no more and no less relative to our everyday practices than our everyday truth claims. Even Todes's convincing description of our background understanding of the vertical field as a *field*—a universal influence flowing down through us—is not a discovery of preconceptionless phenomenology, but, rather, shows the influence of our modern understanding of gravity. Aristotle had no understanding of fields, but presumably experienced his body, not as under the influence of an independent field from which all agents who suitably conform can draw support, but as a material object with a tendency to seek its natural place at the center of the earth—a tendency which upright human beings had to resist.

It looks as though no description of our direct embodied encounter with everyday reality, even if that reality is experienced as independent and inexhaustible, could make the idea of a view from nowhere intelligible. The emphasis on a background of intelligibility correlative with our bodily structure would seem to argue for just the opposite view—a view from *somewhere*, namely from within our embodied embedding. In other words, when we try to describe the other face of objects, that is, the structure of the universe as it is in itself, all we can do is point to boundary conditions independent of us to which we must conform, but how the structure of these boundary conditions is described will always be relative to our vocabulary, practices, and bodily coping abilities.

Clearly, the universe has *some* independent structure and we embodied beings have to get in the right relation to that structure in order to experience anything, but if we can only describe how these boundary conditions affect us embodied beings, we are still stuck in internal realism. How could robust realists possibly break out of the background understanding that makes our everyday encounter with things, as well as any attempt to understand their hidden face, intelligible? But if we can't break out, Rorty and the deflationary realists are right: all our correspondence claims must be internal and redundant.

It might, indeed, have turned out that all we could know about the independent structure of the universe was relative to our current background understanding of the boundary conditions it placed on our embodied activity. But, surprisingly, Galileo and company discovered that we can bracket our direct, embodied experience of the everyday world. We can prescind from the properties of everyday things that depend on our senses, the shape and capacities of our material body, and even our experience of being in touch with an independent reality. We are able, thereby, to discover and investigate a physical universe with no perceptible things with their colors, orientation, solidity, weight, etc.—a universe where there is no near and far, no up and down, and no earlier and later. Moreover, it happily turned out that this deworlding, as Heidegger calls it, was not merely a negative accomplishment, but that, when we bracketed the world of everyday experience, we discovered universal causal laws, and natural kinds, some of whose properties causally explained all the others.

Still, even this discovery could be given an idealist interpretation. Kant argued that what was left behind after our prescinding—the homogenous Cartesian space and pure succession of states that served as the basis of the new science—was still a function of our receptive capacities, so we could never know the boundary conditions as they were in themselves. Pragmatists like Rorty stress that we cannot know things as they are in themselves but must remain confined to our vocabulary for describing things.[10]

Rorty's basic contention is that the description of the universe is up to us, so that, even if there were boundary conditions, we could never know their structure as it is in itself, but only as we conceptualize it. He treats this claim as if it were the consequence of a philosophical argument that the idea of a correct description that corresponds to the structure of the universe makes no sense, but his criticism of Taylor consists in ridiculing the idea that the universe has its own language. And, of course, the universe doesn't speak. But whether there could be a description that corresponded to the essential structure of the universe and was only contingently related to our way of making sense of things is an open question.

Whether the idea of a privileged description of the universe in its own terms *makes sense* is *a philosophical question* that we will argue should be

---

10. Phenomenologists like Husserl, and perhaps Merleau-Ponty, concluded that therefore the laws and entities of science must be abstractions, related to the everyday world like maps to a terrain, in relation to which they get all their meaning. See Edmund Husserl, *The Crisis of the European Sciences and Transcendental Phenomenology*, trans. David Carr (Evanston, IL: Northwestern University Press, 1970). Nominalists like Ian Hacking add that, in order to have anything at all to describe, we must first organize the chaos of data available to our instruments into functionally useful groupings. See Ian Hacking, *The Social Construction of What?* (Cambridge, MA: Harvard University Press, 1999). All share the conclusion that we can never get outside our perceptual capacities, our language, and our practices.

answered in the affirmative. Only then will we be in a position to ask the further question whether *there actually exists* such a privileged description (and whether our science is in the process of discovering it). This question can't be answered by philosophical argument. Nominalism might be right that all the groupings in the universe are imposed by us, but it might turn out to be the case that the structure of the universe has one—or maybe even several—correct descriptions that correspond to its structure. It is crucial to be clear that this is not a metaphysical or a rhetorical question, but an *empirical* one. Much of the apparent plausibility of the deflationary realist view comes from the a priori claim that a description of the universe in itself is an incoherent idea and from the subsequent evaluation of scientific claims from that perspective. We propose to look at the empirical evidence on its own terms.

First, could the universe possibly have its own intelligibility with respect to which our description would be merely our contingent mode of access? We hold that the answer is yes, it could if there were natural kinds with essential properties, and if we could designate a natural kind with a provisional mode of reference that remained noncommittal as to which, if any, of the properties that we used to refer to it were the essential ones. Saul Kripke has defended this view of the possibility of a realistic science by calling attention to the function of what he calls *rigid designation*, particularly the rigid designation of samples of natural kinds.

So, to take two of Kripke's examples, I could start by investigating some shiny gold-colored stuff and eventually find out that its essence is to have an atomic weight of 79, regardless of whether or not it is gold colored. Or, to take another case, I could provisionally identify lightning as a flash of light in the night sky and eventually find out that it is essentially an electrical discharge. Thus, a purported natural kind is first designated by a description that points out an instance of it—that yellow stuff. This pointing fixes the reference but does not commit the designator to the claim that the property used in pointing out the kind is the kind's essential property.[11] In this way,

---

11. We do not believe that the necessity involved in making claims about essences requires claims about David Lewis's possible worlds. Dagfinn Føllesdal, for instance, argues for a form of rigid designation much like Kripke's, but with an even more minimal ontology. For Føllesdal, considerations of "all possible worlds" are resolved into considerations about objects that our language enables us to keep track of although we have many false

the initial description, while relative to our interests and capacities, leaves open the possibility that investigation may discover the thing's essential properties. In this way, Kripke shows that the way demonstrative reference works makes intelligible the idea of our access to natural kinds whose essential properties are in no way relative to our mode of access to them.

Once we are outside the latest version of the mediational picture—that we can know objects only from inside our practices and only through a description based on these practices—and see it as a picture, the idea that we must be trapped inside our mode of intelligibility so that the view from nowhere makes no sense is revealed to be a claim that needs (but lacks) philosophical justification. Then the burden of proof shifts, and the evidence from the progress of post-Galilean science is all the evidence we need in order to claim that we *are* getting a better and better understanding of the boundary conditions that we encounter in perception and which require that we get in sync with the structure of the universe as it is in itself.

This evidence is familiar and once passed for persuasive, but since it has been called into question in increasingly subtle ways from within the inner-outer picture, it is necessary that we review it here.

We have so far argued that (1) we *cope* more and more effectively with the *affordances* offered by the perceptual world; (2) we also get a better and better *conceptual* grasp of the *objects* that surround us; (3) some cultural practices can be seen to be more coherent and less distorting, and thus to supersede others. We now want to add that (4) some accounts of nature provide a better explanation of how the universe works than do others, and that our natural science provides by far the best explanation available.

Let us begin by returning to our everyday coping. When we confront anomalies in our perceptual experience, we know how to find out what's wrong with our current understanding and improve it. If we enter a café that looks much too big for the building it is in, we resolve this anomaly when we see that the walls are covered with mirrors. Then things snap into place, and our confused, partial perceptual grasp becomes clear and secure. Likewise, as we explore a city we gain a more and more perspicuous understanding of it,

---

beliefs about the objects, do not know many of their properties, and do not know how their properties will change over time. Føllesdal "Essentialism and Reference", *The Philosophy of W.V. Quine,* ed. Lewis Hahn (La Salle: Open Court, 1986), 97–115, esp. 107; Saul A. Kripke, *Naming and Necessity* (Cambridge, MA: Harvard University Press, 1980), 15–21.

so that we are no longer surprised and disoriented at each turn. In general, in our everyday perceptual encounters with the world, we are solicited to move towards an ever clearer and more secure grasp of our surroundings.

This supersession built into our perceptual experience can be adapted to give us a robust realist account of natural science. Indeed, it turns out that science has its own internally generated way of progressing. Rather than accepting with Thomas Kuhn that the worlds of Aristotle and Galileo can't be compared because they were asking different questions, we can find specific anomalies that the Aristotelians ran up against that Galileo could account for—for example that missiles from catapults and guns don't head straight for their natural place at the center of the earth, but follow a parabolic path. Or, to take a simpler example (which we invoked in Chapter 3), by assuming that the earth moves rather than the sun, Copernicus could make more sense of the motion of the heavenly bodies than epicycle theorists could, and astronomers could then see that the sun could better be understood as a star rather than as a planet.

The move to a new paradigm is forced on us because the new understanding resolves certain anomalies that plagued the older one. In the light of the new theory, we see the old anomalies as intractable and, although the new theory brings with it its own anomalies, one hopes that these will be resolvable in the long run. Thus the Galilean-Newtonian understanding of inertia allowed us to resolve the intractable paradoxes of "violent movement" which affected the older, Aristotelian view. Since on this understanding, every movement needed to be explained by a contemporary mover, continuous movement required continuing causal power. But in the case of thrown objects, or projectiles, like cannon balls, it seemed impossible to identify any such power. This whole explanandum disappears, and a clear account of all these phenomena can be given, if we move to the inertial perspective, where what needs explaining is *changes* of velocity, and not continuing movement.

Likewise, a culture's background understanding of science can progress. Kepler's success in getting a more complete and clear grasp of astronomical phenomena showed that improvement could be made upon the Aristotelian background understanding that one could not and should not try to account for all phenomena—both terrestrial and superlunary—in the same way. That, in turn, undermined the Greek understanding of science as *empiria*, just as Galileo's findings undermined the medieval idea of *scientia*, and eventually led to the modern understanding of science as *research*. As Heidegger points out, research differs from *scientia* and *empiria* in proposing a *universal* ground plan and then trying to fit *all* anomalies into that plan, rather than just noting anomalies as unnatural events, monsters, or miracles. This new understanding of science as *world picturing*, in turn, gives us a more comprehensive and powerful understanding of nature.[12] More phenomena make more sense, that is, form a more coherent whole, according to the Newtonian ground plan than in the Aristotelian systematization of everyday experience.

In this way, we can see that scientific revolutions are cases of supersession. If they are not immediately accepted it is because the older view is entrenched, not because they are not rationally motivated. The proof is that, once one understands the new overall way of looking at things, in science as in the case of the mirrors on the café walls, there is no way of going back and seeing things in the old way.

Gradually, we are able to develop theories that purportedly correspond to the structures that we had to take account of in our everyday coping. We come to understand that to act effectively, we not only have to resist our body's tendency to fall towards the center of the earth; we see that we have to balance in a field of influence that we come to understand as a gravitational field. We also learn more and more about how our sense organs work and how light and sound energy is propagated, and this, in turn, explains why we have to move the way we do to get an optimal perceptual grip.

Thus, the structure of the independent nature that sets limits to what we can do and supports us when we get in sync with it, is better and better understood by our science, which then feeds back and improves our everyday grasp. This, in turn, confirms our conviction that our science describes the structure of the universe in itself with which our coping is, from the start, in direct contact. But, even if Rorty agreed that our natural science is defined by modes of reasoning which fully justify at least some paradigm changes, such as that from Aristotelian to post-Newtonian mechanics, he would still want to reiterate his claim that we add nothing to all this by saying that the goal of science is to achieve a correct description of the structure of reality; that talk of correspondence is quite otiose.

---

12. Martin Heidegger, "The Age of the World Picture," in *The Question Concerning Technology, and Other Essays* (New York: Harper & Row, 1977), 115–154. See also Jan Assmann, *Moses the Egyptian* (Cambridge, MA: Harvard University Press, 1997).

Perhaps we could understand Rorty's claim by recurring to the follow-ing analogy. Let's say we are watching a group of jazz musicians rehearsing a piece. They play it one way; then one player begins to render his part in a new version; everyone smiles and nods to convey the message: that's much better! Then another player does the same thing, with the same positive result. We can think of these new improvisations as analogous to paradigm changes. And in our example, the changes are unanimously recognized by the participants as being for the better. We can even say that they all share a sense that the performance is improved by them—even that the nature of the piece dictates this.

But now, what would we add by saying that the new version comes closer to the Idea of the music? Or to the music as such? Surely this would just be dressing up what we already know in a sonorous metaphysical garb; it would obfuscate rather than clarify.

Rorty seems to want to say something similar about our science. Even if the move from Aristotle to Newton is, as it were, forced by the rules, that just tells us how we play this game. The game is its own justification; or perhaps if it has a further one, it is that it "works for us" human beings, in the sense of contributing to a healthier, longer, more productive, more pros-perous life. But nothing is added to all this by declaring that the goal of this game is true description of what is really there independent of us.

Now even if "works better" refers us to the increased prediction and con-trol modern post-Galilean science has won for us in a host of areas—though there are many cases of a new theory being accepted, even where there is as yet no technological payoff (and may never be, as in cosmology)—still we normally think of technological control, where it accrues, as a sign that we have got the underlying structure right.

There are two questions here: whether, as our scientific theories advance, we are better able to predict and control phenomena, and whether this is evidence that our theories corresponded to an independent reality. We think it is safe to say that no one doubts that, as scientific theories supersede each other in accounting for anomalies, we also benefit from better and better predictions, as well as opening up new domains where we can better ma-nipulate nature to serve our ends.

It seems harder, however, to get agreement among philosophers that this control shows that our theories correspond more and more closely to the structure of the universe. We would argue that, just as in everyday perception, experiencing more reliable anticipations as we cope signals a better grip on things in the world and how they behave, so, insofar as science and technology lead to better predictions and control in the everyday world, we should assume they are gaining a better grip on the structure of the universe. But deflationary realists can respond that, for pragmatists, control is not evidence for correspondence but simply a kind of spin-off from those scientific theories which we cultivate precisely because they further our interests. Indeed, we generally fund and follow up only on theories that happen to give us control. On this view, rather than control providing a sign that we have got the underlying structure right, what we mean when we claim we have got the underlying structure right is that we have gained more control.

So it looks as though even supersession and control cannot convince those who hold that we can't get outside our language, capacities, and practices—that all intelligibility is necessarily relative to *our descriptions* and what *works for us*—that the progress and power of our science shows that it is homing in on the structure of the universe as it is in itself.

How could one convince them, then? Perhaps nothing can convince someone if he or she wants to remain in the Kantian inside-outside picture. But we can challenge whether the distinction nonrealists are relying on here, between what "works" and what brings us closer to the truth, makes sense of the actual practice of *scientists*.

Let us look at an analogous case: Suppose you are attending the final of the World Cup in Berlin with a companion who comes from those (benighted) parts of North America unfamiliar with the game of soccer. He asks you what's going on, and you reply: "Whichever team puts in what the rules prescribe as the winning performance wins." Your companion feels rebuffed. He could have figured this much out on his own. You can only repair things if you go on to explain what scoring a goal means, and the like. He needs to know the point of the game.

Similarly, if science is a "game," then its point is to find out how the things which surround us, including the factors and forces which impinge on us, really work, which involves defining the laws which govern their behavior. You can't explain this to anyone while avoiding all such words as "true," "correct," "real," any more than you can satisfy your companion in the stadium without talking about "scoring" and "goal."

If all the above considerations fail to move an antirealist reader, let us add one more. Just as the phenomenological description of our direct coping with everyday things shows that we are not imprisoned in our skins or minds, but are open to a shared world, there may be phenomena revealed in our scientific practice that show that our true theories correspond to an independently existing universe.

CHAPTER EIGHT

Plural Realism

AS WE HAVE just seen, in the seventeenth century our culture asked about the structure of the universe as it is in itself independent of all human interpretations and eventually developed a science that claims to be approaching a view from nowhere (Chapter 7). Likewise, thinkers in the West have repeatedly claimed to find behind the plethora of cultural arrangements all over the world an invariant structure, an independent human nature, that could, in principle, be understood by anyone anywhere (Chapter 6). We have attempted to defend these realist claims in Chapters 6 and 7, but any defense must face serious objections which require broadening our understanding of robust realism both in the natural and the human sciences.

We saw in Chapter 7 that Kripke's account of rigid designation enables us to understand how the universe could lead us to discover the meaning of our scientific terms freed from any essential dependence on our meaning-giving practices. But rigid designation has a troubling consequence. It not only allows us to conclude that, insofar as our science discovers the essential properties of the natural kinds, it tells us what these kinds are wherever they exist in the universe; it also forces us to conclude that anyone who correctly uses these natural-kind terms must be referring to these kinds by means of these essential properties. If we have, indeed, discovered the essential property of gold, then it must be true that, even in ancient Egypt, gold had an atomic number of 79. And insofar as meaning determines reference, Kripke's view further implies that whenever the ancient Egyptians succeeded in referring to gold, they were unknowingly talking about a natural kind with an atomic weight of 79.

All of which seems to imply that on the question of the essence of gold, other, earlier cultures that had another view about its nature just got it wrong. Nothing further need be said.

Their views can be put on a par with earlier mistaken theories which have been entertained in the history of Western science, theories which invoked things like phlogiston, or caloric. A substance with the latter name was hypothesized at one time as what underlay heat. It was meant to be a natural-kind term, in the sense that its presence explained the heat of an object, its relative absence the lack of heat. But for the last two centuries or more this has been recognized as a false trail, leading nowhere. It has been consigned to the waste chute of history. And the same would have to be said, say, of the understanding of gold underlying the practice of alchemy in the Renaissance, or of that prevailing in a number of ancient cultures, like that of the Aztecs or ancient Egyptians, in which this precious substance played an important role. We could take a similar stance to earlier understandings of lightning as bolts from the gods, which would be seen as relegated forever by the account in terms of electrical discharge.

But, given that there have been other cultures that open other worlds that may well be on a par with ours, we do not want to accept this implication of Kripke's view. True, for *us*, given our modern Western understanding of nature, an essential property is one that explains how the kind in question falls under a large number of universal causal laws, and these causal laws are understood to be laws that hold everywhere and at all times. But to people in another culture, say the ancient Egyptians, gold's essential property might have been that it was sacred and so shone with divine radiance. How can we accept the claim that true scientific assertions correspond to nature as it is in itself, without accepting the implication of Kripke's scientific realism, that, insofar as our scientific understanding of nature is true, different beliefs about nature held by other cultures must be simply false, that, for example, the Egyptian's understanding that the essential property of gold is that it has sacred powers that cause its radiance is simply mistaken?

To begin to answer this question, we have to remember that ours may well be the only culture that claims that, if true, our theories concerning the kinds of entities in the universe correspond to those kinds as they are in themselves. Other cultures do not ask about the universe as it is in itself, in the sense of modern Western science. They have no notion of a view from nowhere. Only because we have such a notion are we committed to the claim that our definition of natural-kind terms captures the meaning of these terms for anyone correctly using them anytime anywhere.

Of course, our scientific understanding, if true, would be true in the world of the Egyptians even though they couldn't understand it; but it doesn't follow that what they meant by gold is determined by our science. Not that they had a rival universal account "from nowhere" of gold as a natural kind, but neither were they deflationary realists *avant la lettre*. Gold's being sacred presumably was not understood as *relative to their description of it*, but it wouldn't be right to say that they held sacredness to be a universal truth about gold which all must acknowledge. As we move back into the era of truly "polytheistic" cultures, it becomes obvious that the reality is more complicated. Each people has its gods, but it is dimly recognized that other peoples have their own divinities, and there is no temptation to classify these as nonexistent or unreal. This is how the people of the ancient Mediterranean seemed to understand the predicament of religious plurality, which became evident to more and more people in the "multicultural" cities of the ancient world. All except the Hebrews, who made the startling, and to many people offensive, claim that the gods of other peoples were simply inventions, "made by human hands."[1] But the "polytheistic" understanding seems much more widespread among humans. Something like the same sense of a plural ontology of the divine seems to have existed, for example, among North American aboriginals.

It is hard to reconstruct the views of people in these ages, before what seems to us an unavoidable question arose, namely, which among these

1. Margalit and Halbertal make the interesting claim that the earliest condemnation of idolatry in the Hebrew Bible treats other gods as existing; the sin of worshipping them is one of infidelity to the God of Israel, and often understood in the sexual image of "whoring after false gods," whereas later on these rival deities are seen as pure invention (cf. the mockery by Elijah of the prophets of Baal). Moshe Halbertal and Avishai Margalit, *Idolatry* (Cambridge, MA: Harvard University Press, 1992).

different construals of the divine is the right one (including, in the gamut of possibilities, that all are wrong because there is no divine)? Any formulation we might want to give today is going to seem awkward and not quite right. But these earlier peoples presumably sensed that they neither simply *discovered* universal truths about nature and the gods, nor *invented* their description of them, but drew on their form of life to *reveal* reality from their own perspective. They thus implicitly took for granted that the way nature is revealed depends on what Heidegger calls "different kinds of seeing and questioning natural events."[2]

The deflationary realist is right that once world disclosing is recognized it would be mistaken to claim, as Kripke does, that the description of natural kinds that are relied upon in each particular world must either correspond to the single structure of the universe as it is in itself, or be false. But it doesn't follow that one has to give up a robust understanding of correspondence. Our peculiar culture did ask about the structure of the universe as it is in itself independent of all cultural interpretations, and eventually developed a science that claims to be approaching a view from nowhere. All currently available evidence confirms that gold is a natural kind and its essential property of having an atomic number of 79 explains all its other properties that can figure in universal causal laws. True, other cultures could have different understandings of what an essential property is, and other views about what is important about gold, and so pick out other properties as being the essential ones. Any property of gold, even, for example, where it was mined, could be picked out as essential by some culture.

Still, one should not jump to an antiessentialist conclusion. Understanding gold as essentially having an atomic number of 79 does explain, or at least promises to explain, the causal properties of gold. That these causal properties are important to us is only our contingent mode of access to it, so that its atomic number may well correspond to the structure of gold *as it is in itself*. Still, having an atomic number of 79 need not be considered to be *the* essential property of gold. It is essential only relative to our way of questioning nature so as to reveal its independent properties. The Egyptians might well have revealed properties of gold only accessible through their religious practices.

2. Martin Heidegger, *The Question Concerning Technology*, 117.

Thus what gold *is* depends upon a culture's practices. This tells us that the Rortyan pragmatist has got something right: one should not be a modern scientistic essentialist. Our science, if true, tells us the property of gold that accounts for its other physical properties, but this needn't be the whole story. As Heidegger puts it, "The statements of physics are correct. By means of them, science represents something real, by which it is objectively controlled. But . . . science always encounters only what *its* kind of representation has admitted beforehand as an object possible for science."[3] On this view, the Egyptians' understanding of the essential property of gold, if true, could also correspond to or reveal an aspect of nature.

Given our understanding of supersession, we claim that we could, at least in principle, have taught the ancient Egyptians our science, and with it the distinction between the "in itself" and the "for us." They could then see both that gold was a natural kind in our sense with its essential property being an atomic number of 79, and also that our disenchanted understanding of nature overlooks the fact that nature is sacred, and its kinds have a sacred essence our science can't see. Even a view from nowhere of things as they are in themselves is only one limited way of disclosing them. Again, as Heidegger puts it, "What is represented by physics is indeed nature itself, but undeniably it is only nature as the object-area, whose objectness is first defined and determined through the refining that is characteristic of physics."[4]

Thus, while gold's physical property of being untarnishable is *causally* explained by our science in terms of universal laws and its view from nowhere, gold's essential sacred property of shining with divine radiance may only be accessible to Egyptian religious practices. The kind of correspondence claim implicit in the practices of premodern cultures, if spelled out, would then amount to the claim that they have practices for gaining *a perspective* on reality that corresponds to *one aspect of reality* without claiming to have *a view from nowhere* that reveals objective reality *as it is in itself.* The aspect such practices *revealed* might have causal properties that could only be *activated* by those specific practices, and so would not be discoverable by a disenchanted science with a view from nowhere. Hence, what might seem a mystery or even an impossibility from the standpoint of our science might

---

3. Martin Heidegger, *Poetry, Language, Thought* (New York: Harper & Row, 1971), 170.
4. Heidegger, "Science and Reflection," in *The Question Concerning Technology*, 173–174.

have a causal explanation within a given set of practices that reveal another type of causality, alien to our science, at least as we now understand it. The two accounts would be in this sense incompatible. In the most extreme conceivable case, these culturally activated causal properties might even override the causal properties discovered by our science. If confirmed, levitation or extrasensory perception might be such cases. Of course, our unity-based physics would then have to be revised to take account of such phenomena or else be abandoned.

Furthermore, although we don't at present know of any alternative universal theories of nature as it is in itself, there is much we don't understand, and there may be other ways of getting at universal causal properties that our Western science can't grasp. The success of acupuncture has so far resisted all attempts to understand it in terms of Western medicine, and we may simply have to accept two accounts of the body, one in terms of molecules and electrical impulses, and another that plots the paths of a kind of energy that can't be understood by our physics. We may also be seeing signs of a need for two independent accounts of reality, one describing those aspects of nature as it is in itself revealed to detached observers , and another account of reality as it is revealed to involved human beings. Scientists and philosophers have, after all, so far failed to reconcile mechanical theories of physical reality with the seemingly undeniable facts of free will, consciousness, and meaning. Convergence in all these cases would certainly be satisfying and reassure those of us who question nature in a Western way concerning a *uni*verse that our theories describe an independent reality, but we have to leave open the possibility that there is no single privileged way nature works.

All this leads to the conclusion that—although according to our disenchanted science it is true everywhere, whether or not anyone knows or cares about it, that gold has an atomic number of 79 since this property explains all the causal properties our science can see—it is only relative to our disenchanted way of questioning natural events that having an atomic weight of 79 is taken to be *the* essential property of gold. More generally, there is no single essential property of gold. Given the above considerations, where essences are concerned one has be a pluralist.

Once we have broken free of the last version of the inner-outer mediational picture—the claim that we must be imprisoned in our description of reality—we can agree with Rorty that there is no *one* language for correctly describing nature, while holding, contra Rorty, that there could well be *many* languages each correctly describing a different aspect of reality. Our position could then be characterized as *pluralistic robust realism.* That is, there may be (1) multiple ways of interrogating reality (that's the "plural" part), which nevertheless (2) reveal truths independent of us, that is, truths that require us to revise and adjust our thinking to grasp them (and that's the robust realist part), and where (3) all attempts fail to bring the different ways of interrogating reality into a single mode of questioning that yields a unified picture or theory (so they stay plural).

1

It is obvious that we are proposing a position which is going to be difficult to defend, not (we believe) intellectually, but rhetorically in the context of today's culture. There are two powerful positions being defended today—let us call them modern scientism on one hand, and different brands of sub-jectivism and relativism on the other. Each defines itself as one of only two possible outlooks, in mortal combat with the other. Each therefore makes itself look plausible by showing up what is excessive or rebarbative in the other. For scientism, any questioning of the unique truth of modern science must be equivalent to a rejection of truth itself as a category; for Rorty and others, the only way to escape the imperialism of modern science is precisely to question this category.

The line we are taking here upsets this picture, by introducing a third possibility. We are bound to be seen by each extreme as a defender of the other—as scientistic by the Rortyan, and as enemies of truth and science by the followers of scientism. From our point of view, we have to wage a struggle on two fronts, to establish the viability of our position, in its differ-ence from the extremes.

That is what we have been doing in the above pages, showing how the valid claims of modern science to grasp things as they are in themselves do not conflict with the possibility that there are a plurality of revealing per-spectives on the world (nature, cosmos, universe?).

But this position can be attacked from an angle which we have not yet considered. We can be seen as having after all capitulated to scientism. Per-haps modern science can be portrayed as depending on one big unproven assumption, which we have unthinkingly taken on board.

After all, isn't this preference for unity over diversity a Western prejudice? Shouldn't we, like Nietzsche and other nominalists, be suspicious of all unity as what we impose in order to cope? Irresolvable diversity, as in quantum physics, might be better evidence of an independent reality. Even if the need for unity is grounded in the unity of our body and the unified perception correlated with the body (as no doubt it is), doesn't that show that such a preference for unity is just another prejudice we should overcome?

We mentioned above how in earlier stages of human culture, there was a recognition that the gods of others exist which didn't raise the issue of whose conception of the divine was really the correct one. This way of seeing things was relegated to the past, in part through (Jewish-Christian-Muslim) monotheism, but also by the great philosophical developments of the ancient world. Plato and Aristotle build from the understanding that we are trying to understand a single, coherent cosmic system. The step to unity was taken way back then. Modern science inherits this, but gives it a new twist. This lies in the notion that the privileged view is a view from nowhere, beyond all our partial perspectives.

There are also privileged perspectives on reality that don't purport to be a view from nowhere but purport to supersede all other views. They range from Plato's claim that the philosopher has such a perspective once he or she emerges from the cave, to religions such as later Judaism, Buddhism, and Christianity, each of which claim to have a true and universally valid perspective, but have no notion of a view from nowhere.

But even though this understanding of the unicity of the universe is a venerable tradition in our civilization, we might still ask: Is it just a prejudice? We think the answer should be: yes and no. Yes, it is a Western "prejudice," if we mean by this a deeply anchored feature of our worldview. Moreover, it is one which is arguably anchored in our sense of the unity of the body, as we mentioned above. But it is not a "prejudice," if we mean an assumption enframing research which is not itself capable of being established or disproven in the course of this research. That a unifying perspective corresponds to an aspect of reality is supported by the success of our totalizing kind of science (research) and our progress towards the fusion of horizons argued for in Chapter 6. In short, the question of unity and multiplicity is ultimately a matter which must be decided empirically, in the broadest sense of this word, that is, by what turns out to be true at the end of the day.

The proof of this is that on this crucial matter of unity versus multiplicity, the jury is still out. It is indeed the case that the assumption that, if they are true, our seemingly incompatible understandings of reality must converge, draws on the basic way we have of assuring ourselves that we have an optimal grip on everyday reality. We can't be satisfied with two contradictory perceptions, such as that the café we entered is both big and small. But we have to get used to the idea that, while in everyday perception all perspectives on an object must be ultimately unified, both physical and human nature may be accessible from different perspectives that reveal perhaps incompatible, but at least mutually irreducible, essential features of things as they are in themselves.

Even restricting ourselves to our own cultural history, we have passed through phases in which nature was to be cultivated, then dominated, or read as the book of nature created by God, then objectified and exploited, and, currently, seen as a resource to be made as flexible as possible and optimized to get the most out of its possibilities. Now the pre-Socratic understanding of nature as welling up, lingering, and passing away[5] seems to be making a new appearance as the Gaia principle where we understand nature as making a claim on us to be preservers. And the objectified view of nature was already challenged in the poetry of the Romantic period. Wordsworth spoke of

> a sense sublime,
> Of something deeply interfused,
> Whose dwelling is the light of setting suns,
> And the round ocean and the living air,
> And the blue sky, and the mind of man;
> A motion and a spirit, that impels
> All thinking things, all objects of all thought,
> And rolls through all things.[6]

5. Martin Heidegger, *Introduction To Metaphysics*, trans. Gregory Fried and Richard Polt (London: Yale University Press, 2000), 14–16. See also Hubert L. Dreyfus and Sean Dorrence Kelly, "Conclusion: Lives Worth Living in a Secular Age," in *All Things Shining: Reading the Western Classics to Find Meaning in a Secular Age* (New York: Free Press, 2011), 190–223.

6. William Wordsworth, "Tintern Abbey," in *The Complete Poetical Works* (London: Macmillan and Co.), 1888.

Our yes-and-no response to the accusation that the espousal of unity is a prejudice could be summed up in another way. It is true that we are inclined to seek a unified theory of all phenomena; and in this we are pushed perhaps not only by our cultural traditions, but in the very way that we are as embodied beings in the world. The ability to unify two hitherto unconnected theories increases our confidence in both. Thus, just as the repeated failures to find an account of the convergence of physics and chemistry in the nineteenth century raised serious doubts as to the foundations of chemistry, so the evidence that the two sciences converged was greeted with relief as strong evidence of a single independent reality described by each.

We have another important example of this search for unity in the series of attempts to bring into synthesis Aristotelian philosophy and each of the three great monotheistic religions. This started with the Jewish thinker Maimonides, whose work inspired various Islamic thinkers, such as Ibn Sina and Ibn Rushd (Avicenna and Averroes), who in turn influenced the great attempted synthesis of Aquinas. It is interesting to note that the perceived inability to effect a full synthesis led with Ibn Rushd to a theory of "double truth," a relativization of important truths to one or other framework, because understood just simpliciter they seem to clash irremediably. This move has something in common with some modes of modern "antirealism"; we can see its affinities, for instance, with Kant's solution of the antinomies. Aquinas, for his part, espoused an uncompromising *unified* realism, and set himself the task of realizing a full convergence. Whether this succeeded or not is, of course, still very much a matter of dispute in some circles. Kierkegaard, following Pascal's proclamation that the God of Abraham, Isaac, and Jacob is not the God of the philosophers, and reacting to Hegel, the last great unifier, gave convincing arguments why any such attempt must fail.

In sum, our Western commitment to coherence and unity can be seen as a particular perspective from which to study physical and human nature. But it cannot for all that be called into question by general metaphysical views such as nominalism or Nietzschean perspectivism, although its claim to uniqueness and superiority can be.

We don't at present know of any alternative physical theories incompatible with our own, but there is much we don't understand. We mentioned above the case of acupuncture, which has so far resisted all attempts to understand it in terms of Western medicine. We may in the end simply have to accept two accounts of the body, which cannot be combined into one coherent scheme. Resolving them into one could come about in three possible ways. (1) Further study might reveal that these two sciences are dealing with quite different questions, where the answers to one don't impinge in any way on our theories about the other—as some people suggest is the case between the issues of natural science and those of religious faith.[7] (2) One approach might just supersede the other, showing it to be inadequate, unable to resolve anomalies that the better view can handle, as post-Galilean mechanics relegated Aristotle's theory of motion. Or else (3) one science might offer a more general theory, of which the valid findings of the other could be construed as special cases (as Einstein's theory supersedes and includes Newton's laws of motion). Neither (1) nor (2) seems likely as a resolution to the puzzling relation of acupuncture and modern scientific medicine, as we now understand it; the ranges of complaints they treat overlap; and neither seems just wrong. Perhaps a variant of (3) can be conceived, in which a future broader and deeper theory can explain the successes of both as special cases; but nothing like this is even remotely on the horizon today.

And there are worse cases. We may even be seeing signs of a need for two *incompatible* accounts in the so-far-fruitless struggles of scientists and philosophers to reconcile their mechanical theories of physical reality with the seemingly undeniable facts of free will and consciousness. Given the history of theory and of the belief in the unity of reason in the West, convergence in these cases would certainly be satisfying and reassure us that our theories describe an independent reality, but we have to leave open the possibility that there is no single way the universe works. Unless one is committed to unity as a test of reality, such separate realities need not mean that there is no description that corresponds to reality but mean, rather, that there are several.

Such a possibility raises the broader question of whether an account of physical nature as meaningless can be reconciled with an account of the cosmos as having a meaning and human beings having a privileged place in it. An approach to a positive answer takes the form of trying to show that our science supports the Christian view of a human-centered universe. Given that the basis of our science is the discovery of a universe whose causal laws take no account of us and our human meanings, this seems an unpromising

7. See Stephen Jay Gould, *Rocks of Ages: Science and Religion in the Fullness of Life* (New York: Random House, 1999).

strategy. The best it can do is show that our actual universe is highly improbable, but any specific universe would be equally improbable and might give rise to other kinds of conscious beings, and there is no way for our kind of science to explain how the universe could be caused with us in mind.

A more promising approach (analogous to [1] above) is that taken by Dostoyevsky in *The Brothers Karamazov*. One of the aims of the book is to give an existential account of Christian concepts such as guilt, resurrection, and rebirth and Christian sacraments such as baptism and confession, showing how these concepts and practices respond to crucial aspects of the human condition and need not conflict with the laws of physics and chemistry.[8]

For Dostoyevsky, a view of our special place in the cosmos, such as Alyosha's experience in the middle of the book that "there seemed to be threads from all those innumerable worlds of God, linking his soul to them, trembling all over,"[9] is not in conflict with modern science's account of a disenchanted universe. As long as we make no causal claims that contradict our scientific cosmology, such an experience of the meaning of the cosmos and our place in it can be understood as giving us access to a reality in itself that is in no way dependent on our description of it and yet in which human beings have a central place.

The fact that there could in principle be many such irreducible and even incompatible perspectives on reality would, of course, be evidence that there is no *one* way nature is and so no *one* truth that corresponds to it, but it need not mean that there is *no* way nature is in itself—that all natural kinds are constructions relative to our interests as "perspectivists," as Nietzsche and

8. For example, when Dimitri hears about Claude Bernard's discovery of neurons, he mistakenly thinks he has to give up the belief that he has a soul and that he can expiate his crime through suffering. "Imagine these neurons are there in the brain . . . (damn them!) there are sort of little tails, . . . and as soon as they begin quivering . . . I see and then think, because of those tails, not because I've got a soul. . . . It's magnificent, Alyosha, this new science! A new man's arising . . . and yet I am sorry to lose God!" (book XI, chap. 4). Alyosha's response is simply to ignore Dimitri's conclusion and encourage him to discover a different sense of the new man. And soon Dimitri says, "Brother, these last two months . . . a new man has arisen in me. He . . . would have never come to the surface if it hadn't been for this blow from heaven" (book XI, chap. 4) In contrast to the new man of science, which Dostoyevsky doesn't reject, Dimitri's equally valid existential understanding links suffering, resurrection, and joy.

9. Dostoyevsky, *Brothers Karamazov*, book VII, chap. 4.

the postmoderns claim, or, as Rorty seems to hold, that no descriptive per-spective can be true of and justified by the causal structure of reality. Rather, we should conclude that there are several ways of describing nature all of which may be true.

Thus, *pluralist robust realism* can avoid *reductive realism*, which holds that science explains all modes of being, and *scientific realism*, which holds that there is only one way the universe is carved up into kinds so that every user of such terms must be referring to what our natural-kind terms refer to, while yet rejecting *deflationary realism*'s claim that we cannot make sense of true statements in science corresponding to the way things are in themselves.

Once we have overcome the mediational picture, with its ultimately in-valid a priori reasons to invent ever more subtle forms of antirealism, our everyday experience of our direct embodied contact with an independent reality opens a space for a whole range of accounts of our essential nature and of the nature of the universe, thus freeing us for an empirical investiga-tion to determine which, if any, of these accounts correspond to aspects of reality, and, how, if at all, these various aspects fit together.

2

Just as the fact that there are many different ways of understanding reality leads us to question our understanding of physical nature, the multiplicity of cultures, each with their own understanding of what it is to be human, leads us to question our understanding of human nature.

Roughly half a century before Kripke developed his account of rigid des-ignation, Heidegger worked out a similar idea in order to justify his attempt to determine the essential features of what he called the *Dasein* in man. He realized that, if he wanted to talk about the essential features of human be-ing, he could not claim at the beginning of his investigation that he knew which they were. So where should he begin? To solve this problem Hei-degger developed an account of what he called "noncommittal" reference. Such reference, he argued, was made possible by what he called formal indi-cators (*formalen Anzeige*). Noncommittal reference begins by referring to a type of entity provisionally, using only contingent features, and attempts to arrive at the kind's essential features (if it has any), by means of an appropriate type of investigation.[10]

The discovery of formal designation allows Heidegger to begin *Being and Time* with a provisional definition of *Dasein* as the being whose being is an issue for it. Further investigation of the meaning of human practices—Heidegger's hermeneutic method—reveals that *Dasein* implicitly takes a stand on itself by using equipment to fill some role such as teacher or carpenter. Thus, the being that takes a stand on its being turns out to need a sense of what matters so as to take up some specific role, and needs to be absorbed in coping with equipment in order to carry out whatever projects that role requires. Heidegger describes this threefold structure of being-in-the-world as thrown, absorbed (falling), and projection, and shows how this structure enables *Dasein* to open up a world. As the being that discloses a clearing or world, *Dasein* has no essential structure other than the basic structure of being-in-the-world. *Dasein*'s essential structure, then, turns out to be that it is an open discloser of a world.[11]

Later Heidegger sees that this capacity for world disclosure makes it possible for human cultures to disclose different worlds with different styles in each of which human beings are understood as having different natures. Thus, in the West, human beings have been understood successively as nurturers of nature, as the cultivators of all that is, as rational animals, as creatures of God, as subjects over against a universe of objects, or, currently, as optimizing resources in order to get the most out of their possibilities. Each of these accounts, if it is taken as the exclusive account of our essence, covers up the others and occludes the truth that we are world disclosers, but each,

10. See Martin Heidegger, *Being and Time*, trans. John MacQuarrie (New York: Harper, 1962), 152. Here, Heidegger speaks of "a non-committal *formal indicator*, indicating something which may perhaps reveal itself as its 'opposite' in some particular phenomenological context." See also Martin Heidegger, *The Phenomenology of Religious Life*, trans. Matthias Fritsch and Jennifer Anna Gosetti-Ferencei (Bloomington: Indiana University Press, 2010), 42–45. Henceforth we will translate *Anzeige* as "designator" rather than "indicator," to bring out the parallel with rigid designation.

11. Charles Spinosa, Fernando Flores, and Hubert L. Dreyfus, *Disclosing New Worlds: Entrepreneurship, Democratic Action, and the Cultivation of Solidarity* (Cambridge, MA: MIT Press, 1997).

if properly understood as one among many possible ways to be human, confirms that our one essential feature is to be world disclosers and that this essential way of being enables us to understand the role of language as well as the fact that every culture embodies a view as to the point of human life.

Thus, each specific understanding of human nature underwrites a specific understanding of human goods, or of human rights. For example, various definitions of human beings as rational animals point to their respective accounts of human excellence, from Plato's austere notion of a life entirely ruled by reason, through Aristotle's theory of a balance of human goods, hierarchically ordered, in the good life, to Kant's stress on the autonomy of rational agency. Theistic views define our highest good in terms of a certain relation to God. The modern individualist notion of moral order sees us essentially as bearers of rights, and so on.

Heidegger is obviously trying to formulate a crucial feature of human life. But what he points at, that human beings are capable of producing, and actually have produced, very different forms of life, still leaves us with an awkward question. We can't help asking ourselves whether all these life forms rest on equally valid understandings of humanity, in the sense of realizing the highest and best of human potential. Our contemporary world, where very diverse cultures are brought into close contact, and forced to mingle, can lead us to be understanding of differences, and not to bridle at what our forbears would have seen as the "outlandish" customs of others.

Still, not every culture's sense of what is good seems equally acceptable. Viewpoints that condone inflicting gratuitous pain on others, however defined, seem to us to have missed something important about human beings. But mustn't our sense of moral outrage be relative to our cultural commitments? As we survey history and human cultures, we hear a bewildering cacophony of voices, making incompatible claims. Is there any way that various cultural understandings of what is essential to human beings can be ranked and criticized apart from our particular cultural perspective? Is there any hope of our ever coming to a consensus around these issues? Or at least of achieving some modest convergence, perhaps in eliminating some candidates, perhaps in coming to a general agreement that some elements are essential to any definition of the human essence?

We believe that some steps have already been taken in both these directions. First, what we can now at least reconstruct retrospectively as valid supersession arguments have already emerged in human history. We touched briefly on one such argument in Chapter 3. A century and a half ago, women were forbidden the vote in all liberal democratic societies (or societies on the road to liberal democracy, as we now describe them). Only a minority even of women were in favor of giving women the franchise. What seemed at the time terribly convincing arguments supported the status quo against the small, brave minority proposing universal suffrage. Women allegedly lacked the capacity, the judgement, the self-control, and the objectivity, or, given their real role in life, lacked the interest and commitment, to act as citizens. Such arguments have since been swept aside.

But this has not been simply the brute victory of one historical force over another. We wish to speak of rational supersession here because today, thanks in part to the actual experience of women's participation, the various arguments about their essential lack of capacity or interest just seem bizarre. We wonder at the people who put them forward and espoused them, and have trouble believing either in their intelligence or their good faith. In this latter suspicion, we are wrong and anachronistic, but the fact is, these arguments can no longer be rationally advanced. When women were denied certain kinds of responsibility, and confined to other domains of life, beliefs about their capacity or fitness for politics seemed to be confirmed, but now such beliefs fly so much in the face of the everyday, banal facts of our lives that they appear absurd.

In the terms in which Ernst Tugendhat describes supersession, we have been through a "way of experience" (*Erfahrungsweg*)[12] which is irreversible. Before two views were still rationally possible; but now only one is.

An analogous point could be made about the suppression of slavery in our civilization. The peculiar institution relied on certain myths, which could only be believed as long as the actual oppressive situation gave them a color of plausibility. Once this goes, they become literally incredible.

Second, we have seen partial convergences between very different overall views on certain points. Certain aspects of the rights of women are a case in point also in this context. Supersession arguments have wrought changes within civilizations, as in the above examples in the West. But there are also convergences between civilizations. Thus in the Islamic Republic of Iran,

---

12. Ernst Tugendhat, *Selbstbewusstsein und Selbstbestimmung* (Frankfurt: Suhrkamp, 1979), 275.

while there are still severe restrictions on many aspects of women's lives, they have the vote. The reasoning underlying this change has followed a different trajectory from that in the West; it has taken place within an Islamic framework and set of assumptions. But it has come in this respect to something like the same place.

We can see this as part of a more general movement, whereby a possible global consensus on human rights could be building in our world. This convergence would have the status of what Rawls calls an "overlapping consensus."[13] That is, the parties remain in disagreement in their deepest beliefs about human beings, their nature, and their good (what Rawls calls their "comprehensive theories of the good"), but nevertheless can come together in affirming certain norms as right. One can argue that such a consensus has been building ever since the aftermath of the Second World War, through such moves as the Universal Declaration of Human Rights and other such international instruments, through various international interventions in the name of human rights (with all their faults and biases), the International Court at The Hague, and so on. At its strongest, it would never amount to unanimity in religious/ ethical outlook, but rather to a convergence, from out of very different outlooks, and for different reasons, on a certain table of norms.[14]

So the field of difference may be narrowing, not just de facto, as in the case of consumer products, but de jure, as it were; that is, the field of differences may be less than before. And it may be further reduced in the future.

But we can sift this vast field of divergent views in another way as well. We can ask: What elements or insights are so solid that they would have to be incorporated into any view of the human essence and the human good which we could find believable? One such element is perhaps that human beings are world disclosers. But Heidegger's account, as we have just seen, is purposely empty so as to leave open all specific ways that *Dasein* can interpret itself and disclose a world. Are there any specific essential structures beyond the necessarily empty structures of being a world discloser?

If there are, we might hope to find them in the invariant structure of the human body. For help we can to turn to Merleau-Ponty and Todes. As

13. John Rawls, *Political Liberalism* (New York: Columbia University Press, 1993).

14. See Charles Taylor, "Conditions of an Unforced Consensus on Human Rights?" in *Dilemmas and Connections* (Cambridge MA: Harvard University Press, 2011), chapter 6.

we have already seen, Merleau-Ponty has given us a detailed account of the role of the body in perception, especially of how our active body gives us the experience of being in direct contact with reality. But as Todes points out, Merleau-Ponty's account of the body as an "I can"—where this means I can be drawn to move in response to the solicitations of affordances, in order to get a maximal grip on them—does not give us an account of the way our specifically shaped body's capacity for specific forms of movement is essential for our having a world at all. If there are such culturally invariant structures, they may set limits on all accounts of our nature. They might even contribute to the specific content of all acceptable accounts.

Such an approach to finding content that would have to be incorporated into any view of the human essence and the human good in order for us to find it believable, perhaps even intelligible, has barely been explored, but there are tantalizing hints of what it might reveal. We have seen that our upright posture seems to provide a cultural invariant that is reflected in various cultural understandings of dignity and righteousness. It is not clear that we could make sense of a culture in which the "high and mighty" bow or prostrate themselves before the "lowly," or where calling someone upright was an insult.[15]

Another aspect of the universal role of our body, which we've already mentioned, is our sense of having to balance in what Todes calls a vertical field of influence. When he analyzes what is involved in balancing, Todes notes that we have a sense of a force that descends from above and flows though us. Moreover, we are required by the force to align ourselves with it. If we fail to do so, we fall, but if we succeed, we are rewarded by being able to face our tasks and other people and act effectively. Whatever interpretation a culture gives of the place of human beings in a wider reality, it may have to incorporate some sense of having to conform to a power outside our control that requires us to get in sync with it and rewards us when we do. Finally, we have mentioned (in Chapter 6) our sense of intercorporeality, namely

15. The intelligibility of going against this pervasive sense of the meaning of high and low cannot be taken for granted. Any such action has to be highlighted and given special significance, as Jesus does in the New Testament (Mt 20:24–28; Jn 13:13–15). But it is a testimony to the pervasive power of our sense of the meaning of up and down that no culture, even our Christian one, has been able to institutionalize the lowliness of those who have the highest authority.

that, given the way our bodies work, our perceptions and actions are directly linked to those of others from the moment we open ourselves to the world.

It may be that any ethical sense of the good, and any moral sense of the right, and especially any religious sense of indebtedness to a power beyond our control, has to conform to these essential features of our specifically human form of embodiment. Todes planned to work out a phenomenological argument for just such a claim but died before he could carry it out. Whether such a claim can be sustained in detail remains to be seen, but there can be no doubt that our upright posture plays a pervasive role in shaping our world and distinguishing our way of being from that of the animals. The idea certainly deserves further investigation.

3

If we look at history in a longer perspective, we can perhaps descry a certain convergence. For example, what have been called the "Axial"[16] revolutions brought about analogous changes in different world civilizations, so that we can see some affinities between philosophy in the age of Plato and Aristotle, on one side, the teaching of the Hebrew prophets in ancient Israel, the new thinking we associate with the name of Confucius in China, the new teachings of the Upanishadic thinkers, as well as those of the Buddha and other reformers in ancient India. These great changes seem to exhibit common features: a new universalism, a critical stance to previous religious life, the introduction of higher notions of the good, and a focus on individual religious and moral development. Not only did these developments define, each

16. *Achsenzeit.* See Karl Jaspers, *Vom Ursprung und Ziel der Geschichte* (Zürich: Artemis-Verlag, 1949). Even the civilization which seems most to have avoided the Axial turn, the Japanese (cf. Robert N. Bellah, "The Heritage of the Axial Age: Resource or Burden," and Shmuel Noah Eisenstadt, "The Axial Conundrum between Transcendental Visions and Vicissitudes of Their Institutionalizations: Constructive and Destructive Possibilities," both in *The Axial Age and Its Consequences*, ed. Robert N. Bellah and Hans Joas [Cambridge, MA: Belknap Press of Harvard University Press, 2012]), has gone through a ratchet effect, insofar as it has been influenced by post-Axial religious forms (Buddhism, and to some extent in recent centuries Christianity). These have been to some degree neutralized, but that is still different from living in a world in which the issues raised by the Axial transformation have not yet been raised.

in its own context, what came to be seen as a higher form of life, but they also irreversibly changed the societies in which they occurred.

This brings us to what one might call "ratchet effects,"[17] that is, transitions in history in the aftermath of which people find it impossible, or even inconceiveable, to return to the previously reigning outlook. The Axial turns were undoubtedly of this type. But we can think of others: for instance, the move to state-centered and urban societies, and more recently, the steady progress of industrialization, state-building, and globalization. But unlike certain paradigm changes in science, such as that from Aristotelian to Newtonian mechanics, and some less broad changes within our ethical outlook of the kind we discussed above, they leave behind them a sense among many moderns that, while something has been gained, something else has been perhaps irretrievably lost.[18] It is difficult to imagine how it could be otherwise.[19]

These changes all involve convergences, but just as in the case of human rights, the coming together reflects continuing irreversible diversity. The world consensus on human rights seems valid to many people, but for very different reasons in different milieu. Some will ground the right to life on a view of humans as made in the image of God, others on the Buddhist principle of *ahimsa*, others on the Kantian notion of the dignity of humans as rational agents, others again on the utilitarian principle of avoiding pain. We are no closer to consensus on our deepest underlying reasons. We may agree that we have made progress, for instance, when we sign a new convention on human rights, but we disagree profoundly on what this progress consists in: Are we realizing the dreams of the eighteenth-century Enlightenment, or coming closer to the will of God, or going further on the path of the Buddha?

This reflects the relation we see between the different Axial revolutions. There is an undoubted affinity between the teachings of Plato, the prophets of Israel, and the Buddha, for instance, but there remain deep differences of basic ontology.

17. Charles Taylor, *A Secular Age* (Cambridge, MA: Belknap Press of Harvard University Press, 2007), 273.

18. See Pierre Clastres, *La Societe Contre l'Etat* (Paris: Minuit, 1974). The changes of the Axial age are discussed in Taylor, *A Secular Age*.

19. See Gopal Sreenivasan, "What Is the General Will?" *Philosophical Review* 109, no. 4 (2000): 545–581.

4

We can see on both the scientific and cultural-ethical levels, that we have good reasons, moral and intellectual, to press forward and attempt a unification of perspectives, but also good reasons not to be too sanguine about our prospects. It is this predicament to which our robust but plural realism does most justice. This is not by any means a dogmatic belief that no unification is possible, just a healthy suspension of judgment about its ultimate possibility, along with the recognition that further unification is well worth trying— and even, for some of us, a faith that pushes us to go on trying.

Index